Collins need to

Guitar

Collins need to know?

Guitar

All the tips, techniques and
inspiration to get playing

David Harrison

The author would like to dedicate this book
to his students, who taught him to teach.

Special thanks to Heather and Dexter

First published in 2004 by
Collins, an imprint of
HarperCollins*Publishers*
77-85 Fulham Palace Road
Hammersmith, London W6 8JB

The Collins website address is:
www.collins.co.uk

08 07 06 05 04
6 5 4 3 2 1

A catalogue record for this book is available from the British Library

Created by: harrisonresearch
Editor: James Harrison
Designer: Nick Withers
Musical supervisor & CD production: Guy Dagul
Photography: Matthew Ward
Guitarist (b&w) photographs: Dave Peabody
Cover design: Cook Design
Front cover photograph: Daniel Norman/istockphoto

ISBN 0 00 719088 3

Colour reproduction by Colourscan, Singapore
Printed and bound by Printing Express Ltd, Hong Kong

contents

Introduction	6
getting started	14
your first songs	24
strumming patterns	42
starting to pick	52
using bar chords	72
further techniques	92
music notation	110
music – in theory	124
a world of styles	148
guitar essentials	174
Glossary of terms	182
Need to know more?	185
Index	186
CD track listing	190
Acknowledgements	191

Introduction

It's no secret that playing a musical instrument is one of the greatest pleasures yet dreamt up by humankind, and having decided to learn the guitar, you are already well on the way to discovering the joy of music for yourself.

This book is here to help you every step of the way, from buying a guitar, to tuning it and holding it correctly, through to strumming, picking, accompanying, soloing, writing your own songs, reading music and expanding and refining your musical tastes.

The playing techniques are based on a guitar programme run by the author at a large London Institute attended by upwards of 70 students in various classes there. This book is an adaptation of these classes – classes that have been honed and revised to get people playing quickly and confidently without skimping on any important information.

We start off by choosing the guitar that is right for you; then we get playing; once you are confident with the guitar and conversant with the basic concepts, we look at some theory and notation to give you the best possible chance of reaching your musical potential; and finally, the idiosyncrasies of different guitar styles and techniques are explored, closing with the chords at-a-glance, glossary and tips for further study.

What's in this book?

The bulk of the material in this book is concerned with guitar techniques, and nearly all of that is illustrated with musical examples. These generally take the form of well-known songs written out using conventional chord symbols with a guide to strumming and picking, and you will learn more about these symbols as you go. Many of the examples can also be found on the accompanying audio CD, and you will be able to play along as you work through the book.

Playing vs. practising

You will also learn to distinguish between playing and practising. There is an old saying in music that practice should always sound dreadful: that way you can be sure that what you are practising is something you need to be working on. If you are practising and it sounds fine, it's time to move on to something with which you are struggling. For this reason, you should set aside some playing time: time to sit with the guitar and just enjoy playing.

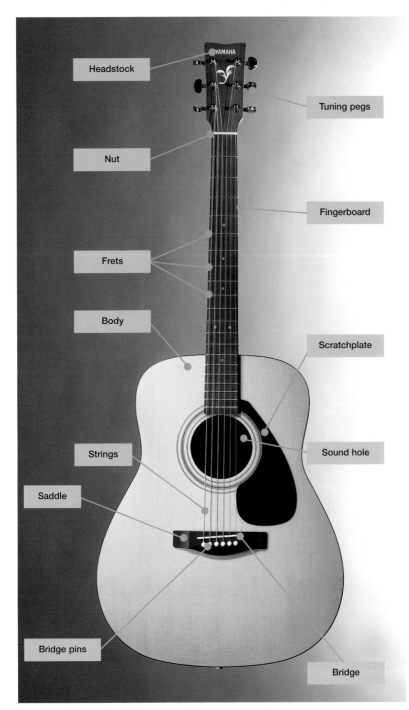

Headstock

Tuning pegs

Nut

Fingerboard

Frets

Body

Scratchplate

Strings

Sound hole

Saddle

Bridge pins

Bridge

◄ The basic parts of a Western acoustic guitar – these apply equally to the classical (or Spanish) style guitar too.

But make sure you don't confuse that with your regular practice sessions.

You should be practising, uninterrupted, quietly, slowly, methodically, and alone, every single day. Not for too long: a 20 minute session will suffice if you really are just practising and not messing about. If you can spare longer, then so much the better, as long as you stay focused and enthusiastic.

Take pride in your practice: you might like to keep a diary, with notes on what you have achieved and what still needs work, or you might like to tape yourself, once a week, just to remind yourself how much progress you are making. Remember that people who are struggling with playing a song often play it too quickly, on the

▲ An electric guitar headstock showing the machine heads. On Fender-style guitars the machine heads are all mounted on one side.

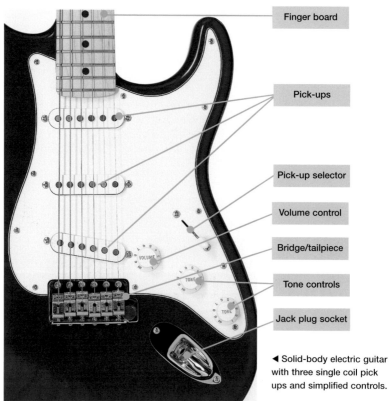

Finger board

Pick-ups

Pick-up selector

Volume control

Bridge/tailpiece

Tone controls

Jack plug socket

◀ Solid-body electric guitar with three single coil pick ups and simplified controls.

◀ A good music store should be an excellent place for choosing, restringing and servicing your guitar and accessories. It should also be the helpful signpost to local tuition, second-hand gear and first stop support network.

grounds that the mistakes don't last as long. It is actually sometimes harder to play a song slowly, as you are then forced to play cleanly, precisely and deliberately. Any song will sound fine (and in some cases best) if played very slowly - as long as it is played crisply and accurately. It's down to perseverance and courage.

Chord symbols & diagrams

When you are playing the songs in this book you will be spending a lot of effort on reading the chord symbols and the lyrics, then yet more effort on translating that into finger positions and sounds. One useful approach is to memorize the songs, if only section by section, and if only temporarily, so that you can concentrate more easily on sequences of positions and sounds. Eventually, because these songs all have structure, melody, lyrics and rhythm, they will more or less remember themselves – that is to say that each chord and lyric will link to the next chord and lyric.

But to begin with, try playing a few bars without looking at the page and you might be surprised how much your confidence will improve. And of course the more songs you remember the easier it becomes to remember songs. People who have learnt hundreds, or even thousands, of songs by heart often say the first 50 were the hardest to learn.

▲ Close up of a Western guitar fingerboard. The circular dots on the neck and fingerboard are position markers to help you find your chords quickly.

Learning the music

All the songs in this book and on the CD are folk songs of one sort or another. They were all composed a long time ago, and have remained popular because they have memorable melodies and are easy to play. And the thing they all have in common is that they are in the public domain. This means that you can write them down and play them without any fear of infringing copyright.

Rooted in folk music

Folk music is at the heart of popular music, and various styles discussed later in this book – including reggae, blues, bluegrass, and country – are themselves types of folk music. All of the pieces in this book and CD have been covered by well-known folk, pop, rock or blues musicians and you will find many versions available on record. Often this music has been handed down from one generation to another aurally, and each successive playing adds something to the music. For this reason, you will find many

▼ This book covers many different guitar styles – as amply demonstrated by three quite different guitar virtuosi playing in unison here: Bert Jansch (centre), folk-baroque guitarist (who co-founded Pentangle with John Renbourn), with Johnny Marr (right) (ex The Smiths and The The) and Bernard Butler (left) (ex-Suede), his guitar being a Gibson ES 335, a classic blues/rock guitar.

'versions' of most of the songs that appear in this book, and many different ways of playing them. That goes for the chords, too. Because folk music is constantly being adapted and is not always studied in an organized way, many chord shapes have more than one fingering, but this book indicates the fingerings that over the years have emerged as the most efficient, or most comfortable, or most logical (not always all three together!). Even if you have already learnt to play certain chords in a way that conflicts with the fingerings shown here, you might like to try them for a while, especially since the trick isn't so much in playing chords as in changing from one chord to another – and that's why these fingerings have been selected.

Whatever style you are playing, whether heavy rock, acoustic folk, pop, country, or jazz, or anything in between, the basic techniques displayed in this book, and illustrated in the chosen songs, apply equally well. Finally, remember, it is a 'teach yourself' type book, and you will not only be the student, but also the teacher. So you will have to learn to be patient, diplomatic, encouraging, disciplined and inspiring to yourself. Good luck, get playing and enjoy!

▲ The author David Harrison in relaxed playing mode. Remember to distinguish between playing time and practice time. Aim for 20 minutes a day, every day, if you really want to crack the techniques of guitar playing without tears and tantrums.

The CD
How to play & play along
On the CD you'll find all the songs in the book plus some of the other instrumental and tuition pieces in two versions: one to repeat and practise; the other more for fun playing along in a karaoke style. Tracks are counted in with a click. These clicks give the 'tempo' of the song. This CD will really bring the tuition to life and help you grasp the fundamentals in an easy-to-follow style.

How to use this book

Several special diagrams and charts are used in this book, and you need to familiarize yourself with them before you start. There are chord diagrams, chord symbols, picking and strumming diagrams and tablature and music notation. Any words you don't understand are also explained in the glossary.

Chord diagrams and photographs

The chord diagrams show you exactly where to place your fingers. Below are a diagram and photograph for the chord C. Familiarize yourself with the way these work and how they relate to the guitar neck.

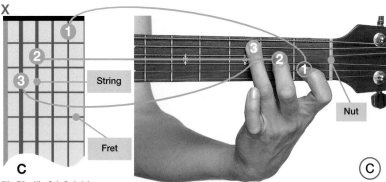

C

6th 5th 4th 3rd 2nd 1st
String number

▲ Notice how the diagram is turned upright: the thick line at the top represents the nut. The circles represent positions for fingers, and the numbers within them show which left hand finger should be used. The X indicates that the 6th string should not be played. Compare the orientation with the photograph, which shows the same chord.

▶ Example of a picking pattern used in the book.

Strumming patterns

You will be learning strumming patterns, and these are also shown by diagrams (see below). They indicate the direction of the hand movement below each beat, and the slashes (/) show when the fingers come into contact with the strings to strum. In this example, you are strumming 5 times: on the 1st beat (down); on the 2nd (down); then immediately up; then up again after the 3rd beat; and finally after the 4th beat.

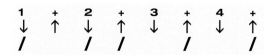

Picking patterns

You will come across picking patterns later. They are represented by diagrams like the one below.

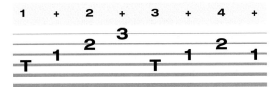

The line of numbers along the top of the chart show the beats (often subdivided, hence the '+' sign). The larger numbers refer to the right-hand fingers that are used on the strings. In this example, the thumb picks the 4th string on the 1st beat, followed half a beat later by the first finger on the 3rd string, and so on.

Songs

Finally, the songs themselves are written out in a format that you will find in most song sheets. The chords to be played are written above the lyrics, and the number of beats after the first strum of the chord is shown with a slash (/).

𝄞 This symbol helps you find the first note of each song (should you want to sing along).

⬤ **Track 14** ⬤ **Track 15**
How to play   Play along

▲ These symbols lead you to the appropriate track on the accompanying CD.

◀ Example of a picking pattern used in the book.

▶ Simplified chord diagrams are sometimes used for chords that have been shown before (this is the C chord).

▲ A piece of music written both as notation (top) and tablature (above) which you will come across later.

◀ Example of a song used in this book. The first A chord is played for a total of three beats (the strum plus the two '/' beats). The upright lines represent bar lines – the end of one bar and the beginning of the next.

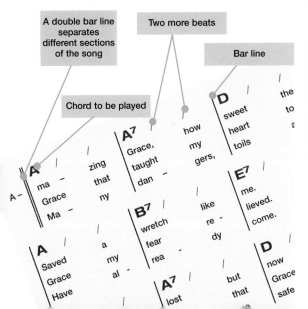

A double bar line separates different sections of the song

Two more beats

Bar line

Chord to be played

getting

started

Buying a guitar can be an exciting experience, though not a little intimidating for the beginner. In this next section we'll take a look at a few different styles of guitar – from acoustic to electric – and the varied accessories you might need, and then we'll get your guitar tuned up and ready to go.

Choosing a guitar

There are many different types of acoustic guitar and they break down into two main groups: steel-string and classical. With electric guitars it's down to personal taste and pocket.

▲ The classical, also known as the Spanish, guitar is an acoustic instrument with nylon strings. The nylon strings give a delicate tone. Notice the neck joining the body at the 12th fret.

Guitar types

The steel-string (or Western) guitar generally has a slightly larger body and always has steel strings, giving a more biting, twangy sound than a classical guitar. It's what many people think of when they say 'folk' guitar, and especially when the word 'acoustic' is used in rock and pop music. Good examples of the steel-string guitar sound include James Taylor, Bob Dylan, or John Renbourn.

The classical (or Spanish) guitar has nylon (previously gut) strings, and a smaller body, giving a warmer, mellower sound. Traditionally used to play classical music, this type of guitar is also used for Latin American styles such as the bossa nova, and many folk singers prefer the gentler sound: the guitar accompaniment of Bob Marley's Redemption Song, for instance, is a classical guitar. Willie Nelson has used the classical style guitar sound to great effect.

Which one?

Either type of guitar is tuned the same way and has the same number of strings. The neck of a classical guitar usually joins to the body at the 12th fret, while on a steel-string guitar this is generally around the 14th fret, but unless you are playing all the way up the neck (and you certainly won't be to begin with) this is not a consideration. The classical guitar neck is wider than the steel-string guitar, and some people find that the fingers need to reach a little further to find the right positions: at the beginning this

◄ Make sure you visit a shop with a wide range of guitars where you can sit quietly and try out as many as you want. Concentrate on the sound (rather than the look) of the guitar, and make a decision based on what your ears (rather than your eyes) tell you.

can be a bit of a strain. On the other hand, some beginners find the tighter strings of a steel-string guitar can be much harder to push down and prefer the softness of the classical nylon strings.

A steel-string or classical guitar is equally suitable, as long as it is in reasonable condition. Any cracks in the wood should be stable, the tuning mechanisms should turn smoothly, and the distance between the strings and the fingerboard should not be so high that it is difficult to press the strings onto the neck. This distance is known as the 'action', and one cause of high action can be a warped neck, which should be avoided at all costs.

Electric and other styles

Although you could learn to play on an electric guitar (and many people do), you will require an electric amplifier and for a beginner this can become noisy, cumbersome and expensive. The sheer portability of an acoustic guitar is – along with the beautiful sound – one of its greatest attractions. Twelve-string guitars, although fun to play and great to listen to, are not for the beginner. Nor are arch-tops (a jazz style guitar), and resonators (including 'Dobro' guitars) are specialised instruments that require specialised techniques. If in doubt, get an experienced guitarist to advise you.

▼ An electric guitar is less portable than an acoustic guitar as it requires an amplifier which also costs more money.

All about strings

Most guitars are sold ready-strung: that is, with strings already on. Strings will need regular maintenance – including cleaning and replacing from time to time. But the most important things that strings will need is tuning, which we'll be exploring soon.

New strings

Tuning can be quite a painstaking and frustrating process – especially if you are not used to hearing whether a string is slightly too low (flat) or too high (sharp), but your ears will eventually become accustomed to discerning small differences in pitch (how high or low a note is). The key here is patience. Be prepared to put in a bit of practice – and remember to use your ears all the time. New strings tend to go out of tune quite quickly but soon they will settle and become 'played in'.

Gauges

Steel strings come in different thicknesses, known as 'gauges', and the shop will advise you which is right for your guitar. The six strings in a set will all be different thicknesses, and a set is named after the thickness of the thinnest in the set, measured in hundredths of an inch: .010, for instance, would indicate a very light gauge, where .013 or .014 would be heavy. Most people will require something like a .011, or medium light, to start out. Thicker gauges can produce more volume but can be very tiring on the fingers. Light strings, on the other hand, have more 'give', and are especially suitable for bending notes and very delicate playing, but create problems of intonation, especially for the beginner.

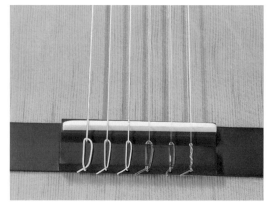

▶ Notice how the nylon strings of a classical guitar loop through and over the saddle on which the bridge sits.

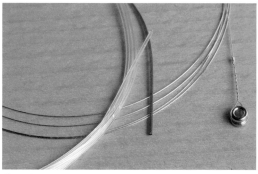
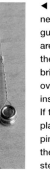

◄ Steel strings should never be put on a classical guitar, and vice versa. If you are not sure, check how they are attached to the bridge – if the string loops over itself, then the instrument is nylon strung. If there are white or black plastic pins, called bridge pins, slotted into the bridge, then it is going to be a steel-strung guitar.

Stringing service

Many stores nowadays offer a stringing service for a time after you have bought a guitar. Whether you have chosen a steel-string or a classical guitar, you ought to change the strings every few months. New strings give a brighter, more musical sound, but can be very difficult to keep in tune at first as they have a lot of stretch in them. They tend to calm down after a few days and should give you long service, but eventually they will become dirty, dull and worn and will need to be replaced. This is a job for a professional, as it's easy to get into a mess if you haven't done it before.

Let the shop do it the first couple of times, and take a close look at the way the strings are put on, especially with regard to the way they are connected to the tuning pegs at the end of the neck. Steel strings should never be placed on a classical guitar, and vice versa.

MUST KNOW

Restringing

If you feel confident enough to re-string your own strings this is shown on page 179

◄ Aside from breaking, strings take a lot of wear and tear, and need care and cleaning to keep the tone pure and the tuning accurate. See page 178 for string cleaning.

Accessories

It can be hard to separate out all the bits and pieces on offer for beginning guitarists: tuners, picks, cases... what do you really need and what can you do without? Here we'll sort out the must-haves from the don't-needs.

Cases

The most important piece of kit after the guitar is a case, and these come in two styles: hard and soft, and both offer some level of protection. Hard cases can be used for transit on airplanes or for long-term storage, but they are heavy and awkward to carry. A soft case will protect your guitar against the everyday scuffs and scrapes and is ideal for carrying around to class, rehearsals or gigs. And soft cases generally have pockets for all those other nick-knacks that we're about to discuss.

Picks

Picks, or plectrums, can be an unnecessary complication but for certain styles are indispensable. They come in all sorts of shapes and sizes, with some specialised picks for particular styles. They can be worn on the thumb, or on the finger-tips, but are more usually held between the thumb and fingers. The point is, you can do with your right-hand fingers everything that you might want to do with a pick to begin with, whether picking or strumming – and the fingers are much more versatile. Unless you are concentrating on a style where a pick is absolutely necessary, such as electric rock, or jazz, try to give them a miss for now. Drink some milk and grow those nails! Given the wide array of extras on the market, it's easy to get carried away with buying this or that accessory, but none will improve your playing on its own.

MUST KNOW

What else?
If you are intending to learn to play classical music and want to adopt the correct posture you should invest in a footstool, and you'll soon find a music stand useful.

Straps

Many people find that a guitar strap helps to keep the guitar in position when sitting, and of course a strap is a must if you are standing. There is a huge variety of straps out there, but they all do pretty much the same job and style is a matter of taste. Comfort should be your first priority here, especially if you are standing, as guitars can get heavy after a while. For certain guitars it might be necessary to have buttons installed to attach the strap – most guitar shops will do this for a nominal charge.

Tuners

You'll find it essential to have some way of tuning your guitar. Some people use tuning forks or pitch pipes (that produce the note you need) to make the sound of the note to which your strings should be tuned, but electronic tuners are now available. Inexpensive and fool-proof, an electronic tuner 'listens' to the strings of your guitar as you pluck them one at a time and tells you whether you need to raise or lower the pitch to tune them. Be sure to read the manufacturer's instructions before you start. Adjustments are usually indicated by a needle or lights on the tuner. Brilliant! Try the internet also for tuning aids such as www.bangingsticks.com

Metronomes

A device that keeps a steady beat can be a valuable asset for guitar practice, as it encourages you to hold a constant rhythm as you play, enabling you to resist the powerful temptation to slow down and speed up. There is also a huge variety of 'play along' tapes and CDs that do a similar job, but the metronome is a time-honoured and much respected method. If you find it tricky to keep a steady beat, the metronome might be just the thing.

▲ Straps

▲ Pitch pipes

▲ Electronic tuner

▲ Capos, or capodastres, and how to use them are covered in more detail on pp.88-91.

Tuning your guitar

Tracks 1-6
Tuning

For the guitar to sound the way it should when you play it, the strings need to be tightened (or loosened!) to exactly the right tension. This is known as tuning.

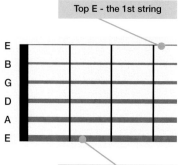

Top E - the 1st string

E
B
G
D
A
E

Bottom E - the 6th string

▲ The six guitar strings are known by the letter-names shown. You'll notice that both the bottom and top strings are called E – it may be a bit confusing at first (see page 30).

There are various ways to tune your guitar, all with the same result, but which ever way you choose, it might be wise to seek the help of someone you trust who has experience of tuning until you feel confident enough to try it yourself. The biggest cause of broken strings is over-tightening, and if you don't know what you are doing, you could get into a fix.

Tuning with a sound source

You will need some kind of sound source, such as the opening tracks on the CD accompanying this book, or a piano, or a tuning fork (make sure it's a low E, not the more common A), or a pitch pipe, to begin tuning. Whatever sound source you use, begin by playing a low E – this is the note to which the sixth string should be tuned, and you'll work up through the strings to the thinnest as you go. Having tuned the 6th string, you will use that note to tune the 5th string, and then the 5th string will be used to tune the 4th, and so on. See the diagram opposite.

MUST KNOW

Pluck the string
When adjusting the tension of the strings, it's a good idea to pluck the string first, and then start turning the tuning peg. Keep the string sounding all the time that you are turning the peg.

Tuning by the frets

The diagram below shows how to tune each string from the previous one: having tuned the 6th string from a tuning fork, piano, pitch pipe or other sound source, put your finger on the 5th fret of the 6th string to give you the sound of the open (no fingers) 5th string. The open 5th string should sound the same as the 6th string fingered on the 5th fret.

▼ The 5th fret of a string is usually the same note as the next string up – the exception being the relationship between the 3rd and 2nd strings (on this occasion it is the 4th fret).

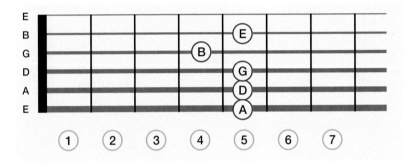

Now tune the open 4th string by playing the 5th string fingered on the 5th fret, and so on. Always play the 5th fret on the previous string except when you are tuning the 2nd string – in this instance you will need to finger the 3rd string on the 4th fret.

Remember to to pluck the string first before you adjust the peg, this way you will know if you are turning the peg the right way, and you will also know whether you have turned it far enough. If the sound dies away, just pluck it again. You should never turn the pegs without hearing what effect it's having on the strings. The tuning mechanism on the headstock of the guitar controls the tension, and turning it away from you should tighten the string.

Have a good look at the way the strings are attached, and in what order, so you can remember which tuning peg (or 'machine head') controls which string.

want to know more?

Take it to the next level...

Go to...
▶ **Your first songs** – pages 24–41
▶ **Strumming patterns** – pages 42–51
▶ **Start to pick** – pages 52–71

Other sources
▶ **Your local music shop**
   a great starting point for further study; become a regular and pick up tips and tricks from the helpful staff
▶ **Music stores**
   a huge selection of CDs, DVDs, videos, music magazines, books etc. is out there
▶ **Internet**
   visit www.bangingsticks.com for tuning and more information

your first

songs

Learning how to hold the guitar and keeping a good posture is essential for comfortable, accurate playing, and now we'll show you how. Then it's time to make a start on your first chords and strums before playing through some great popular songs.

How and where to sit

Before you get playing, it's important to look at the way the body and the guitar relate to each other. After all, you are going to be spending quite some time with your guitar so you might as well get comfortable with it.

▲ This is an ideal stool for practising, with or without crossing your legs.

Are you sitting comfortably?

Clearly, if you are going to sit (and you should) you need a chair that has no arms, and you need a chair with a seat that is high enough for your lap to be level, or to slope slightly down away from you. Most chairs are too low to sit on with a guitar – your feet touch the ground too soon and the lap slopes up, causing awkward problems of posture. The best chair is a bar stool, with a rail that your feet can rest on. Alternatively an adjustable piano stool is good. A sofa is not suitable.

Using a mirror, have a good look and feel at the way your arms attach to your shoulders.

▶ Ideally you might like to set up a special guitar corner with your chosen chair, a music stand, a guitar stand and a tape recorder to record your playing. Remember whatever you sit on, resist the tendency to hunch or allow a slouch to creep in.

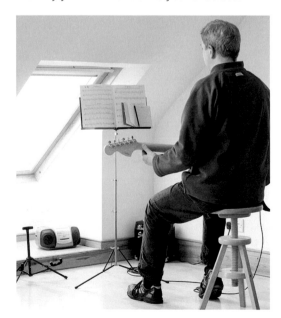

POSTURES

• Let the arms loosely hold the guitar – a guitar will rest on your right thigh, and is held in place by the left hand with the neck resting between the thumb and fingers.

• Whether you are using a chair or a stool, try crossing your legs, right over left ❶ ❷. In any case you should not need to grip tightly with either arm.

• If you have a classical guitar, you might like to try a traditional classical posture ❸ on a standard chair that puts the guitar body between the thighs with the left leg raised by a special little footstool: in this case the guitar should be held reasonably stable without the need to grip with the left hand.

▲ You should be able to hold the guitar comfortably without any appreciable movement of the shoulder blades – no hunching. Place your backside towards the front of the seat of a standard dining chair, let the shoulders relax, look right ahead with a straight neck – no slouching. Try doing this first without the guitar, then with it.

Hand positions

Let's have a look at the hand positions. The right arm drapes over the body of the guitar so that the front edge of the guitar nestles in the elbow. Although it may feel awkward at first, try to let the thumb of the left hand rest on the back of the neck and not 'peep' over. This ensures better reach.

▲ A recap of the finger numbers you'll need to memorize for later right-hand techniques (see page 54).

Right-hand technique

The hand position is best described as being similar to a large crab that has just been picked out of a rock pool – the fingers should dangle loosely in front of the sound hole (see picture below). This basic hand position is good for whatever right-hand technique you will be using, be it picking, strumming, playing lead and so on.

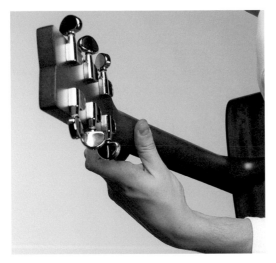

◄ Use a mirror that's big enough for you to see what your left hand is doing – otherwise you will be spending a good deal of time peering over the neck of the guitar to see what's going on and you might get neck and back pains through hunching and slouching. With a mirror you can sit comfortably upright and still get a good view of your left-hand thumb position.

▲ A recap of the left-hand finger numbers you'll need to memorize for later chord positioning (see page 12).

Left hand

The left hand is critical, and its correct positioning is often taken for granted by many guitarists. You will see Willie Nelson wrap his thumb right around the guitar neck, and Eric Clapton, and a whole host of other very fine guitarists grapple with the neck this way. It is common to let the thumb slide up the back of the neck so it 'peeks' over, but you should really try to avoid this. Remember, with the thumb placed at the back of the neck, the fingers can reach much further and more comfortably than if the thumb is peering over the top of the neck.

It's easy to forget, but not hard to do – don't let the thumb pop up. Keep the thumb down, directly behind the second fret, for the most comfortable posture, the least cramp, the best angle for the fingers, and the longest reach.

Try to make sure that your fingertips come down onto the strings as near to right angles on the fingerboard as possible. This will be much easier if you remember to keep your left thumb in the correct position as you will be able to reach much further than if you let your thumb slip around the neck.

▼ Left-handed guitars are readily available. If you are having trouble finding one that you like, you can always have a right-handed guitar adapted. Just get a professional to set the guitar up so that the strings are in reverse order, and hold the guitar the other way around.

The ups and downs

Which way is up? Now, just before we get going, let's familiarize ourselves with some conventional terms for the guitar – especially concerning the words 'up' and 'down'.

The strings

If you thought 'in' and 'out' were confusing in cricket, you ain't seen nothing yet. On the guitar it's like this: the string that plays the lowest note – the thickest string - is called bottom E, or the 6th string. This is known as the bottom string, or the lowest string, even though – when the guitar is being played – it is the furthest from the ground. The one that is closest to the ground sounds highest so it's called the top string, or the highest string – and is also known as the 1st string. You might find it easy to visualize a number 1 as being thin, and a number 6 as being round and fat.

Left hand

Now: if you are asked to move your left finger *down*, you will be moving it in the direction of the lowest string (that is, towards bottom E), and if you are asked to move a finger *up*, it will be towards the highest string. As long as you bear in mind that we are always talking about the sound rather than the physical position, you'll be fine.

If, however, you are asked to move your left fingers *up* the neck, you will be moving it towards the body of the guitar, and if you are going the other way you will be going *down* the neck.

Right hand

And, just to confuse the picture a little more: if you are strumming (which you will be soon) with your right hand, you will be moving *up* and *down* a lot, and this time *down* really means *down*, and *up* really means *up*.

So far, then, we have three different directions for down, and three for up, and that should be enough for anybody. You will just need to remember whether we are talking about the left hand ('down' means up), the neck ('down' means along) or the right hand ('down' means down) and 'sorry' doesn't really seem to cover it. This sort of thing doesn't happen on the bassoon!

First chords

Well, finally we're ready. You've learned
the names and numbers of the strings,
and finger numbers, and fret numbers
too, so it's time to put it all together to
play some chords.

What's a chord?

At the beginning you'll mostly be playing chords,
rather than individual notes. Chords are
combinations of notes all played at the same
time, and this is done by forming chord shapes
with the left hand according to chord diagrams.

Take a look at the chord diagram on the right.
This is the chord of A minor 7, (abbreviated to
Am^7). In this shape you are being asked to place
the first finger of the left hand onto the 1st fret of
the 2nd string; and your second finger onto the
2nd fret of the 4th string.

Notice how the 6th string has an 'X' above it,
indicating that this string should not be played.
This means that this chord uses 5 strings and we
can refer to it as a 5-string chord. You will find it
useful to remember how many strings each
chord uses when you come to strum and pick.

To make a sound with this chord, simply
stroke gently across the strings over the
sound-hole with the thumb of the right hand,
starting with the 5th string and continuing over
to the 1st. This is a basic strumming technique.

Here's another shape: D^7. See how if you
go to D^7 from Am^7 you don't have to move
your 1st finger. This time the 2nd and 3rd fingers
are both used, with the 2nd finger on the
2nd fret of the 3rd string, and the 3rd finger
on the 2nd fret of the 1st string (top string).
D^7 is a four-string chord, as it doesn't use the
5th and 6th strings.

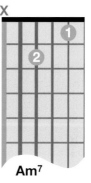

Am^7

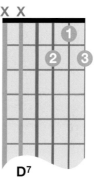

D^7

MUST KNOW

4, 5, or 6 strings
Nearly all the chords
in this book use 4, 5
or 6 strings. Try to
make a point of
learning the number
of strings for a chord
when you learn
each new shape.

Swing low...

Track 8
How to play

Track 9
Play along

Your first song. Elvis Presley, Eric Clapton and Johnny Cash have recorded it, and it's a great favourite with England rugby supporters. Here's your chance to sing along as you play.

Practise slowly, play clearly

Aim to play the chords as cleanly as possible. Practise changing slowly from one chord to the other until you can do it smoothly. Gently strum down with your thumb at the beginning of each bar and let it sound as long as you can before changing to the next chord. Of course, you'll need to leave time at the end of each bar to change, as it's important to play the new chord at the *beginning* of the new bar – and in bars 6 and 7 you should change halfway through too.

Correct fingers for playing the simplified G

Be sure to use the correct fingers on the chords, and keep the 1st, 2nd and 3rd fingers on standby while playing the G chord so you are ready to play the D straight after it.

▶ Try changing from D to A7 without taking the 3rd finger off the 2nd string. Notice how it slides into place as it moves from the 3rd fret to the 2nd fret. Easy does it...

(D)

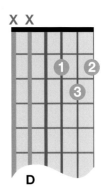

D

A⁷

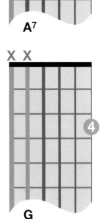

G

D / / /	**D** / / /	**D** / / /	**A⁷** / / /
low, sweet	cha-ri - ot,	coming for to carry me	home. Swing
Looked over Jordan,	what did I see,	coming for to carry me	home. A

D / / /	**G** / **D** /	**D** / **A⁷** /	**D** / / /
Low, sweet	chariot,	coming for to carry me	home. I
Band of angels,	coming after me,	coming for to carry me	home.

Swing

How many strings?

D and G are 4-string chords whereas A^7 is a 5-string chord. Remember to leave out the 5th and 6th strings on D and G, and omit the 6th string on A^7.

♪ For singers, the first note of the melody is an F#, the 2nd fret on the 1st string.

Mirror image
At the moment you might be finding it tricky to see what your left fingers are doing without craning your head over the neck. Try sitting in front of a mirror: you can keep an eye on your left hand whilst retaining your posture – and you get to pose a little too!

(A⁷)

(G)

◄ The chord of G is very common but is a bit of a handful to begin with, so we're going to use a simplified version for now. This one only uses four strings whereas the full version uses six strings (see page 38).

Drunken sailor

This is a favourite sea shanty, for which there are at least 20 verses. If you want to sing more you can 'Sling 'Im in the long boat 'til he's sober', or 'Shave his belly with a rusty razor'... and if you want to hear how it should sound, listen to the Chieftains' version.

Track 10
How to play

Track 11
Play along

Just two chords

This time there are just two chords, one of them a minor, or 'm' chord, Dm, and C. Notice how the 1st and 2nd fingers are in the same place relative to each other in both chords. When you change from one chord to the other, try to keep the shape of these two fingers intact as they move up or down a string. Again the emphasis should be on changing smoothly from one chord to another, and you can afford to play this song as slowly as you like to achieve a relaxed changeover.

When changing between these two chords, make sure you keep the 1st and 2nd fingers in the same position relative to each other. When you move the fingers, they should be 'glued' together so they automatically land in the right place.

MUST KNOW

Smooth change
The trick isn't in playing the chords, it's in changing from chord to chord. Smooth changing means smooth playing.

▼ The little 'm' denotes a minor chord. Compare this with the D chord on page 32. Get familiar with this minor chord and changing to a major chord.

Dm

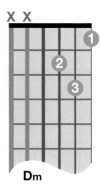

Dm

Dm / / /	Dm / / /	C / / /	C / / /
What shall we do with the	drunken sailor	What shall we do with the	drunken sailor
Hoo - ray and	up she ris - es	Hoo - ray and	up she ris - es

Dm / / /	Dm / / /	C / / /	Dm / / /
What shall we do with the	drunken sailor	Earl- aye in the	mor- ning?
Hoo - ray and	up she ris - es	Earl- aye in the	mor- ning

Remember to land on the new chord at the *beginning* of the bar. As with the first song, strum down once with the thumb at the start of each new chord, allowing yourself enough time at the end of the chord to change to the next one.

Fingers at right angles to the fingerboard

When forming these chords, take great care that your fingers are coming down at right angles to the fingerboard. It's easy to touch more than one string with each fingertip by mistake, so you'll need to be precise. Keep the thumb down to give yourself more room to manoeuvre.

This song was originally a work song, so it needs a strong, regular pulse. Try counting 1, 2, 3, 4 out loud as you play through this song to ensure a strong, rhythmic feel.

If you want to sing, the first note of the melody is on the 2nd fret of the 3rd string, an A.

C

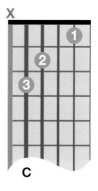

C

He's got the whole world

This old spiritual has been sung by everyone from Nina Simone to Loretta Lynn and it's a great way to practise changing between two common chords: C and G⁷.

Track 12
How to play

Track 13
Play along

The chord of G⁷

This song introduces a single new chord, G⁷. You might find it a bit of a stretch at first, but you will soon get used to it as long as you remember to keep your thumb in the middle of the neck and not wrapped around it.

Start with the C chord and move the 1st finger up to the top string before moving the 2nd and 3rd fingers together down to the 5th and 6th strings. Familiarize yourself with each chord shape thoroughly before practising moving slowly from one chord to the other. The C and G⁷ chords are often used together, and have very similar shapes so this is a good change to practise regularly. Do it slowly. Listen to the way G⁷ creates a need to lead to C, and C sounds happy to rest there. This is known as the Dominant-Tonic Relationship and is discussed later on pages 79 and 132.

MUST KNOW

Left-hand thumb
It's easy to forget to keep your thumb in the right place. Correctly positioned it will allow your fingers to reach comfortably round. If you're not sure how to hold the left hand have another look on pages 28 and 29.

▼ Practise the finger positions of G⁷ as shown.

G⁷

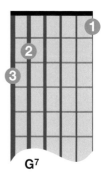

G⁷

He's got the	**C** / / /	**C** / / /	**G⁷** / / /	**G⁷** / / /
	Whole world,	in his hands, he's got the	whole world,	in his hands, he's got the
	Wind and the rain,	in his hands, he's got the	wind and the rain,	in his hands, he's got the

C / / /	**C** / / /	**G⁷** / / /	**C** / / /
whole world,	in his hands, he's got the	whole world, in his	hands. He's got the
wind and the rain,	in his hands, he's got the	whole world, in his	hands.

For now all you need to know is that these two chords very often appear together because of this relationship. For this song, try strumming down on the 1st beat *and* the 3rd beat of each bar, for a steady, regular rhythm.

With all the information on the page in front of you, it can be quite confusing if you have to look up at the next chord every bar and check the picking or strumming pattern. You have to take your eye off the guitar, and it can be difficult to get things to flow. A great way of simplifying the process is to memorize the chords of the song – try learning 4 bar blocks to begin with (practise reciting them without looking) – and you'll be surprised how much more you can concentrate on accuracy, timing, and smoothness.

🎼 For singers the melody begins on the 3rd fret of the top string, which is a G.

MUST KNOW

The pick-up

This song, like several others that we're looking at, has a melody that begins before the first beat of the first bar. This is known as a pick-up (in classical circles it is called an anacrusis) and generally, if one verse has a pick-up all the others will too. Look at the second verse of 'He's Got The Whole World'. It begins 'He's got the wind and the rain' – notice how these lyrics actually begin at the end of the previous verse.

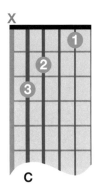

X

C

Down by the riverside

Check out Jimmy Smith's Hammond organ recording, or the gospel version of the Blind Boys of Alabama, to get a feel for this rhythmic gospel classic.

Track 14
How to play

Track 15
Play along

The full G

Now we are getting serious… This song introduces the full chord of G, for which we played a simplified version in the first song. If you have got to grips with G^7, you shouldn't find it too hard to add the 4th finger onto the 3rd fret of the top string to play the full G.

It might prove a challenge until you get the hand position comfortable. Remember – the thumb is the key. Keep the thumb behind the neck and you should have plenty of reach. Some people struggle a little at first with the 4th finger, because it lacks strength. After a few days of regular practice, you'll start to see progress. Persevere!

To strum this song, try playing all the strings of the chord on the 1st beat (G = 6 strings, D^7 = 4 strings, C = 5 strings, G^7 = 6 strings), and then strum across just the top three on the third beat (the middle of the bar) for contrast.

For singers, the melody for this song begins on the open 2nd string, a B.

MUST KNOW

Playing the full G
To begin with you might find it easier to follow this sequence: play C, move out to G^7, and, while removing the 1st finger, place the 4th finger on the 3rd fret of the 1st string to complete the shape.

▼ This is the version of G we are using. It uses the 2nd, 3rd and 4th fingers and feels initially harder to play.

(G)

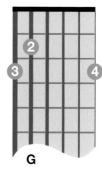

G

G / / /	**G** / / /	**G** / / /	**G** / / /
I'm gonna	Lay down my	heavy load,	down by the	river - side

D⁷ / / /	**D⁷** / / /	**G** / / /	**G** / / /
Down by the	river - side,	down by the	river - side. Gonna

G / / /	**G** / / /	**G** / / /	**G** / / /
Lay down my	heavy load,	down by the	river - side.

D⁷ / / /	**D⁷** / / /	**G** / / /	**G⁷** / / /
Down by the	ri - ver -	side.	Ain't go - nna

C / / /	**C** / / /	**G** / / /	**G** / / /
Stu -dy war no	more, ain't go - nna	stu -dy war no	more, ain't go - nna

D⁷ / / /	**D⁷** / / /	**G** / / /	**G⁷** / / /
Stu - dy	war no	more.	Ain't go - nna

C / / /	**C** / / /	**G** / / /	**G** / / /
Stu -dy war no	more, ain't go - nna	stu -dy war no	more.

D⁷ / / /	**D⁷** / / /	**G** / / /	**G** / / /
Down by the	ri - ver -	side.	

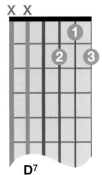

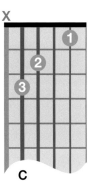

D⁷   **C**

◄ Some books show G played this way, with the 1st finger down on the 5th string. It might at first feel more comfortable, but this version stores up trouble for later. For instance, changing from this version to C is quite convoluted and involves moving every finger a long way. With our preferred version, that change becomes much more logical and, with practice, much quicker. Stick at it you'll be glad you did when you try picking, hammer-ons, and bass runs later with this chord.

John Brown's body

Sung to the tune of The Battle Hymn Of The Republic, this song dates from the American Civil War.

Track 16
How to play

Holding the G shape

This song, another exercise for G, should help you to sustain the shape over a period of several bars. Concentrate on playing slowly but precisely. We introduce three new chords, too: B⁷ and Em. You should aim to change from G, to B⁷, and then on to Em without removing your 2nd finger from the 2nd fret of the 5th string. Try playing just bars 11 and 12 until you can change smoothly through all three chords. Another new chord is Am, a very common chord. Compare this shape to that of C – only the 3rd finger is in a different place.

Track 17
Play along

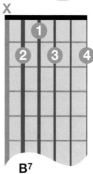

B⁷

Em

Am

B⁷

Em

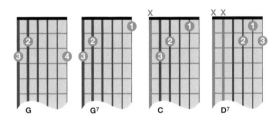

G /	G /	G /	G⁷ /
John Brown's	body lies a	mould'ring in the	grave
Glo - ry,	glo - ry ha - lle	lu -	jah,

C /	C /	G /	G /
John Brown's	body lies a	mould'ring in the	grave
Glo - ry,	glo - ry ha - lle	lu -	jah,

G /	G /	G B⁷	Em /
John Brown's	body lies a	mould'ring in the	grave but his
Glo - ry,	glo - ry ha - lle	lu -	jah, his

Am /	D⁷ /	G /	G /
Soul goes	march - ing	on.	
Soul goes	march - ing	on.	

G   G⁷   C   D⁷

◀ The chords of G, G⁷, C and D⁷, which you have already learnt, are used in this song.

Try strumming slowly and sedately at the beginning of each bar (twice in bar 11 of course), focusing on letting the chords ring out as long as possible.

The melody begins on the 3rd fret of the 2nd string. This is a D.

(Am)

want to know more?

Take it to the next level...

Go to...
▶ **Strumming patterns** – pages 42–51
▶ **Starting to pick** – pages 52–71
▶ **Using bar chords** – pages 72–91

Other sources
▶ **Your local music shop**
   a great starting point for further study; become a regular and pick up tips and tricks from the helpful staff
▶ **Guitar lessons**
   whether private lessons or group classes a weekly diary date will focus your study
▶ **Music stores**
   a huge selection of CDs, DVDs, videos, music magazines, books etc. is out there

strumming

patterns

Having mastered some of the basic chord positions with your left hand, it's time to work with the right hand. Strumming – stroking across the strings – is one of the most important of all guitar techniques and is found in all styles. Although a plectrum can be used, we are going to study a more versatile technique using the fingers and thumb.

Strumming

Strumming is the most common rhythmic technique for playing guitar chords and is found in all sorts of guitar styles. Strumming is especially suitable as an unobtrusive accompaniment to a song, but with correct handling, it can be very powerful and dynamic.

Thumb & finger strumming

Some people strum with the thumb, and others use a plectrum, or pick. The technique we are going to follow here uses the thumb and fingers. Let your elbows, fingers and thumb remain relaxed. The backs of the fingers stroke across the strings as you move the hand down, and the thumb strokes across the strings on the way up. This means that you are only ever using the backs of your nails and – if you bite your nails or if your nails aren't strong – this can be much less strenuous than using the underside of the nails.

Imagine you are holding something smooth and fragile, like an egg, in your right hand – the hand should stay in that position. Notice how the fingers and thumb remain relaxed throughout, brushing quite gently against the strings.

The down stroke

Steps 1-4 (right) are the down strokes of the strum. ❶ the hand is in position just over the sound hole, and then the wrist turns a little to send the fingers down ❷ which brings the backs of the fingernails in contact with the strings. The wrist continues to turn ❸ as the hand reaches the bottom of the down stroke. At the bottom of the stroke ❹ the fingers and thumb are still in the same position relative to each other, and you are now ready to bring the hand back up.

▲ ❶-❹ = ↓ (down stroke). None of the movement comes from the elbow – it's all in the wrist. Try strumming on an Em chord making all six strings ring out.

▶ ❺-❽ = ↑ (up stroke). Remember, although the hand moves up and down continuously as the wrist rotates, only make contact with the strings when you want a strum to be heard.

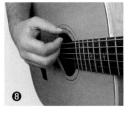

The up stroke

Steps 5-8 (below, left) are the up strokes of the strum. On the up stroke ❺ the wrist rotates back, so that the thumb strokes up over the strings. The thumb continues to stroke over the strings ❻ until the hand eventually reaches the top of the stroke ❼, ready to begin another down stroke ❽. This movement, up, down, up, down, just keeps going along to the beat of the music.

It will take a little while to feel comfortable doing this, but this style is extremely versatile and can be used for just about any rhythm. This will give you the flexibility you need to tackle strumming patterns in a rhythmic, supple way.

Strumming patterns

The diagram below shows a strumming pattern. The top row of numbers are the counts (you could try saying 'one and two and three and four and' out loud to a steady beat as you strum). The arrows show the direction the hand should move: remember - the hand moves up and down in a regular beat whether or not the fingers actually touch the strings. The bold slashes indicate that a strum is sounded at that point.

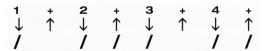

The bottom line of symbols shows the actual strumming pattern. Strum down with the fingers on the first beat of the bar, bringing the hand silently up again ready to strum down (with the fingers) on the second beat. Having strummed down, you should strum up with the thumb halfway through the second beat before a down strum on the third beat with the fingers. The third and fourth beats are identical to the first and second beats. Play the whole pattern smoothly for the 'ching, ching-a, ching, ching-a' rhythm.

We shall overcome

This song began as a work song in slave times and became an anthem of the Civil Rights Movement in the USA in the 1960s, when it was given new words. It was recorded and popularized by Pete Seeger who toured the country with it.

Track 18
How to play

Track 19
Play along

Right-hand techniques

Having spent some time looking at the left hand and a whole bunch of chords, we're going to concentrate on right-hand techniques for a while. Just one new chord is introduced - E⁷. Take a look at the following strumming pattern.

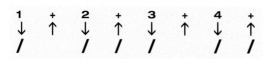

▼ Some people play the D chord with the 1st finger on the 1st string and the 2nd finger on the 3rd string, but most play it the other way around as shown in the diagram.

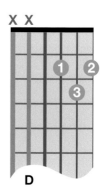

Now try strumming down with the backs of the fingers on the 1st beat of the bar, and again on the 2nd beat, followed immediately by an up strum with the thumb halfway through the 2nd beat. The pattern repeats for the second half of the bar. At the end of every down stroke with the right hand, it's important that you remember to bring the hand back up, even if you aren't strumming an up stroke.

MUST KNOW

The off beat
In this song the beat is divided into two. You play a down stroke on the beat, and the up stroke *halfway* through the beat on the + (the 'and') which is often known as the off beat. Incidentally, the first and last beats of each bar are known as the down beat and up beat respectively.

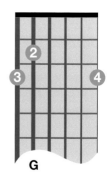

D /	G /	D / / /	D /	G /	D / / /
We shall o - ver		come.	We shall o - ver		come.
We'll walk hand in		hand.	We'll walk hand in		hand.

D /	A⁷ /	D /	E⁷ /	A⁷ / / /	A⁷ / / /
We shall o - ver		come	some-	day - - -.	Oh -
We'll walk hand in		hand	some-	day - - -.	Oh -

G / / /	D / / /	G / / /	D / /
Deep in my	heart,	I do be -	lieve that
Deep in my	heart,	I do be -	lieve that

D / / /	A⁷ / / /	D /	G /	D / / /
We shall o - ver	come some-	day.		
We shall o - ver	come some-	day.		

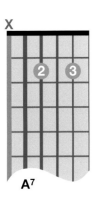

A⁷

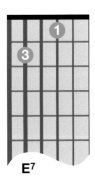

E⁷

Keeping it smooth

The strumming hand should be going up and down all the time like a motor, even if the hand isn't making contact with the strings on every stroke. Aim for a regular up-down-up-down movement, strumming down or up with the fingers or thumb as the pattern dictates. And remember – take it slowly, and make it smooth.

♪ The melody starts on an A: 2nd fret, 3rd string.

E⁷

O sole mio

Track 20
How to play

Track 21
Play along

A famous Italian song – the melody was also used for Elvis Presley's 'It's Now Or Never'. The original lyrics are actually in a Neapolitan dialect and even some Italians find it hard to understand. The rather less lyrical English translation is as follows: 'There is no other sun more beautiful. My sun is on your forehead.'

Introducing the E chord

Just one new chord again, an E – compare this shape to Am, and you'll see that they are identical but on different strings.

This time the emphasis is on the up beats. Try and emphasise the up strokes to give a more dramatic flavour to the rhythm.

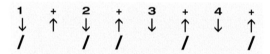

On the second beat, try starting the strum slightly early and drag the fingers down across the strings a little slower than normal – this will give a slightly 'Latin' feel to the pattern.

𝄞 The first note of the melody is a high E, the open top string.

MUST KNOW

Regular strums
The hand should look as though it is constantly strumming even if no sound is heard during certain strokes. Whether the song has three or four beats in the bar, the beat itself generally divides into two – down and up. Make sure you are always going down on the beat and up off the beat.

▼ The E chord.

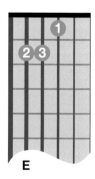

E

E / / /	E / / /	B7 / / /	B7 / / /
Ma n'atu ‖ so - le	cchiù bello, oje	ne' - -	O so - le

B7 / / /	B7 / / /	E / / /	E / / /
Mi - o	sta 'nfronte a	te - - !	O

Am / / /	Am / / /	E / / /	E / / /
So - le,	O so - le	mi - o	sta 'nfronte a

B7 / / /	B7 / / /	E / / /	E / / /
Te - - ,	sta 'nfronte a	te!	

Muscle memory

Finding the chords isn't hard if you've got plenty of time, but when you're strumming along to a song the chords can seem to come pretty quickly. As already mentioned, memorizing the chord progression can really help to prepare you; and allow yourself enough time to change towards the end of the previous bar so that you arrive bang on the beginning of the new bar with the new chord. The single best thing you can do, though, is to practise changing from one chord to the next and back again until it is smooth. This way you are building up what is called 'muscle memory' – your fingers will literally remember what each chord feels like.

B7

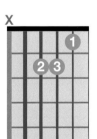

Am

MUST KNOW

Smooth strumming

It can take a little while to get the up-down-up-down motion going smoothly. You could try moving the hand without the guitar and calling out 'Down' or 'Up' on the strokes where you are asked to strum. So for this rhythm you would call 'Down, Down-Up, Up, Up'. This way you get a feeling for the smooth hand movement and an idea of the rhythm at the same time.

Amazing grace

Track 22
How to play

Track 23
Play along

This popular hymn, from the 1760s, was written
by John Newton. He had a religious conversion
after surviving a violent storm as captain on
board a slave ship. Endlessly versatile, it has
been a hit for Aretha Franklin and Elvis Presley.

Strumming pattern

This song has three beats in the bar – you might
think of this as a slow 'bom-ching-ching'. We'll
now try to emulate that feel with the following
strumming pattern.

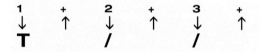

On the first beat of each bar, the thumb will play
the bass note of the chord (6th string for E^7, 5th
string for A and A^7, 4th string for D), followed by
standard down strokes on the 2nd and 3rd beats.

    This style of strumming pattern is much used
in country music where it emulates the sound of
a double bass on the first beat of the bar. Check
out Jim Reeves, Johnny Cash or Hank Williams.

    ♪ The melody for this song begins with an E.
That's on the 2nd fret of the 4th string.

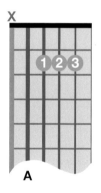

A

(A)

◀ After playing A, strum A^7
and listen to the difference
between them. It's the 7th
that makes the music flow
to the chord of D.

A / /	A⁷ / /	D / /	A / /
A – ma – zing	Grace, how	sweet the	sound, that
Grace that	taught my	heart to	fear, and
Ma – ny	dan – gers,	toils and	snares I

A / /	B⁷ / /	E⁷ / /	E⁷ / /
Saved a	wretch like	me.	I
Grace my	fear re -	lieved.	How
Have al -	rea - dy	come.	'Tis

A / /	A⁷ / /	D / /	A / /
Once was	lost but	now am	found, was
Prec - ious	did that	Grace a -	ppear, the
Grace has	brought me	safe thus	far, and

A / /	E⁷ / /	D / /	A / /
Blind but	now I	see.	('Twas)
Hour I	first be -	lieved.	(Through)
Grace will	lead me	home.	

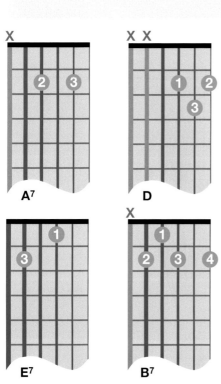

A⁷ D E⁷ B⁷

want to know more?

Take it to the next level...

Go to...
- ▶ **Using bar chords** – pages 72–91
- ▶ **Further techniques** – pages 92–109
- ▶ **A world of styles** – pages 148–173

Other sources
- ▶ **Your local music shop**
  a great starting point for further study;
  become a regular and pick up tips and
  tricks from the helpful staff
- ▶ **Guitar lessons**
  whether private lessons or group classes
  a weekly diary date will focus your study
- ▶ **Internet**
  visit www.allmusic.com or
  www.cyberfret.com for all your needs

to pick

Now that you are getting a feel for the right hand, this section concentrates on finger picking. Here individual strings are plucked with different right-hand fingers. Like strumming, this is an essential right-hand technique and forms the basis of many guitar styles.

▶ Basic picking

Picking (also called finger-picking) individual strings is
a popular alternative to strumming across all the strings
of a chord. Done well, picking can create a very subtle
sound ideal for accompanying a slower song, but it can
also be used in up-tempo songs to provide a driving,
rhythmic backing.

Finger and thumb positions

Notice how the thumb is resting on the bottom
(or 6th) string (see step ❶ opposite), and the
fingers are resting on the top three strings. The
little finger is not used in finger-picking. When the
thumb picks, it moves down towards the fingers;
when a finger picks, it moves up towards
the thumb.

▼ By convention the fingers
are numbered according to
the diagram below. The
thumb is generally shown
as 'T'.

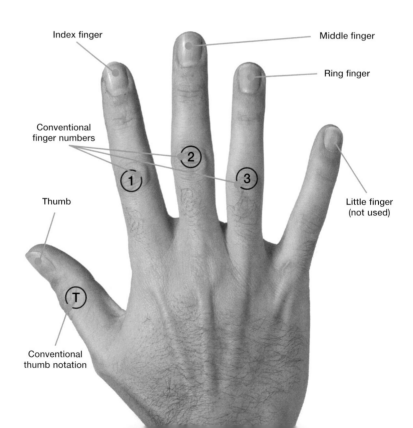

Index finger

Middle finger

Ring finger

Conventional
finger numbers

②

①　③

Thumb

Little finger
(not used)

Ⓣ

Conventional
thumb notation

The basic picking technique steps 1-3. ❶ The picking hand in the ready position. ❷ The thumb moves down when it picks a string. ❸ The fingers move up when they pick a string.

Finger-picking basics

The thumb will usually pick the bottom note of the chord. This might be either the 6th, 5th, or 4th string, and the thumb should be able to move freely from one string to another. As a general rule, the fingers should be picking the top three strings, whilst the thumb picks the bottom three strings. Later we will see that there are situations where you might want to move the fingers away from the strings they are currently on, but for now the 1st finger should be on the 3rd string, the 2nd finger should be on the 2nd string, and the 3rd finger should be on the 1st string.

Once the finger has picked the string, try to remember to return it to a holding position just underneath the same string, ready to pick again at a moment's notice.

MUST KNOW

Don't rely on the little finger

Some people get into the habit of placing the little finger of the right hand onto the front of the guitar just below the sound-hole when finger picking. Although this can be a very useful prop when you begin to practise picking, it will limit your movement options later on.

STARTING TO PICK

55

▶ Oh Susannah

An old nonsense song from Stephen Foster. Oh Susannah was a hit for James Taylor on his album Sweet Baby James from 1969.

Track 24
How to play

Track 25
Play along

Picking pattern

Now we're ready to put your newly learnt picking techniques into practice. In this song, which has four beats in the bar, either the thumb, or one of the fingers will pick on each beat. The diagram below shows how a simple picking pattern might look.

▼ How to finger F: either shape here works well. In the second version (bottom) you'll need to 'bridge' across the 1st and 2nd strings on the 1st fret. It might seem a bit awkward at first but it's a common way to play the chord

▼ Four-finger version of F without bridging (below) and with bridging (bottom).

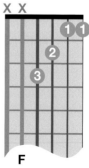

Now I	**C** / / /	**C** / / /	**C** / / /	**G⁷** / / /
	come from A - la -	ba - ma with my	ban-jo on my	knee, and I'm
	Had a dream the	oth- er	night, when everything was still,	I

C / / /	**C** / / /	**G⁷** / / /	**C** / / /
Bound for Loui -si -	ana, my	true love for to	see. It
Dreamt I saw Sus -	ann - ah,	com ing down the	hill. Now the

C / / /	**C** / / /	**C** / / /	**G⁷** / / /
Rained all night the	day I left, the	wea- ther it was	dry. The
Buck-wheat cake was	in her mouth, a	tear was in her	eye. I

C / / /	**C** / / /	**G⁷** / / /	**C** / / /
Sun so hot I	froze my - self, Sus -	ann - ah don't you	cry.
Said I come from	Dix - ie Land, Sus -	ann - ah don't you	cry.

F / / /	**F** / / /	**C** / / /	**G⁷** / / /
Oh, Sus -	ann - ah, now	don't you cry for	me, I
Oh, Sus -	ann - ah, now	don't you cry for	me, I

C / / /	**C** / / /	**G⁷** / / /	**C** / / /
Come from A - la -	ba - ma with my	ban - jo on my	knee. (I)
Come from A - la -	ba - ma with my	ban - jo on my	knee.

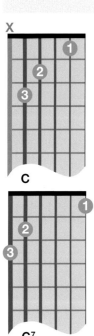

C

G⁷

As you can see, the thumb plays the bottom note of the chord at the beginning of each bar, and the three fingers then follow in sequence, playing the 3rd string with the 1st finger, then the 2nd string with the 2nd finger and finally the 1st string with the 3rd finger. This pattern can be repeated throughout the song.

Remember to play the bottom note of the chord with the thumb each time. For C that is the 5th string, for G⁷ it's the 6th string and for F, the new chord, it's the 4th string. The three left-hand fingers remain on the top three strings throughout. You can play F by bridging across the 1st and 2nd string on the 1st fret. Bridging is pressing two or more strings with the tip of the finger - a 'quickfix' bar chord (see page 74).

♪ The melody for Oh Susannah begins on a C: that's on the 1st fret of the 2nd string.

Danny boy

Track 26
How to play

Track 27
Play along

Listen to Eva Cassidy, Harry Connick Jr. or The Pogues cover of this best loved of Irish songs.

Picking on every half-beat

With this song, the picking pattern gets a little more complex. You'll see from the picking diagram below that you should pick on every half-beat. Thankfully with such a beautiful song it

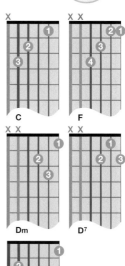

C   F

Dm   D⁷

G⁷

demands to be played at a slow, relaxed tempo. Just bear in mind that as some of the chords last for only half a bar, and the picking pattern lasts for a whole bar, you'll need to begin the pattern again every time you begin with a new chord. In bar 13, for example, begin the bar with C and play the first half of the picking pattern. When you change to Am⁷, play the first half of the pattern again. Remember, in picking patterns if the chord changes before the pattern is finished, start the pattern from the beginning again.

🎼 The Danny Boy melody begins on a B, which is the open 2nd string.

STARTING TO PICK

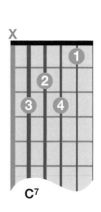

C⁷

C / / /	**C⁷** / / /	**F** / / /	**Dm** / / /
Oh, Danny Boy,	the	pipes, the pipes are call - ing.	From glen to
Come,	and	all the flowers are dy - ing,	if I am

C / / /	**Am⁷** / / /	**D⁷** / / /	**G⁷** / / /
Glen, and	down the mount-ain	side.	The su - mmer's
Dead, as	dead I may well	be,	you'll come and

C / / /	**C⁷** / / /	**F** / / /	**Dm** / / /
Gone and	all the rose - s	dy - ing.	Tis you, tis
Find the	place where I am	ly - ing,	and kneel and

C / **Am⁷** /	**Dm** / **G⁷** /	**C** / **F** /	**C** / **G⁷** /
You, must	go and I must	bide.	But come ye
Say an	A - ve there for -	me.	And I shall

C / / /	**F** / / /	**C** / / /	**G⁷** / / /
Back when	summer's in the	mea - dow,	or when the
Hear, though	soft your tread a -	bove me,	and all my

Am⁷ / / /	**F** / / /	**D⁷** / / /	**G⁷** / / /
Va lley's	hushed and white with	snow.	Tis I'll be
Grave will	warm and swee-ter	be,	for you shall

C / **C⁷** /	**F** / / /	**C** / / /	**F** / / /
Here in	sun- shIne or in	sha - dow,	oh Dann -y
Bend and	tell me that you	love me,	and I will

C / **Am⁷** /	**Dm** / **G⁷** /	**C** / **F** /	**C** / **G⁷** /
Boy oh Dann - y	Boy I love you	so.	(But when ye)
Sleep in peace un -	til you come to	me.	

◀ ▼ The new chords C⁷ and Am⁷.

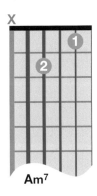

Am⁷

(Am⁷)

Scarborough Fair

Track 28
How to play

Popularized by Simon and Garfunkel in the 1960s, this song dates back to late medieval times, when Scarborough Fair was a huge, 45-day affair.

Track 29
Play along

Two-string picking

Having split the beat in two in the previous song, we are going to continue doing so here. This time, though, you are asked to play two strings simultaneously: on the 2nd beat, pick the 2nd string with the 2nd finger and the 1st string with the 3rd finger. Try to let the top string sustain (keep its sound going) through to the end of the bar, giving a nice ringing tone to the picking pattern.

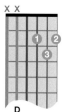

D

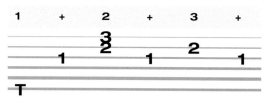

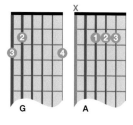

G   A

Once you are comfortable with the picking pattern and can play in an even, measured fashion, try varying the emphasis of the picking pattern from one bar to the next – a subtle change in the strength of each picked note will add a vibrant, organic quality to your playing.

♪ The melody begins on an E: 2nd fret of the 4th string.

▲ D, G and A which you have already learnt.

▼ Your new chord Em.

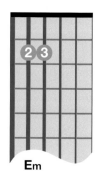

Em

Em / /	Em / /	D / /	Em / /
Are you	going to	Scar – bo - rough	Fair?
Tell her to	make me a	cam – bric	shirt.

Em / /	G / /	Em / /	A / /
	Pars – ley	Sage, Rose –	mar – y and
	Pars – ley	Sage, Rose –	mar – y and

Em / /	Em / /	Em / /	Em / /
Thyme.			Re –
Thyme.			With –

Em / /	G / /	G / /	Dsus / /
Mem - ber	me to	one who lives	there.
Out any	seams nor	need – le	work.

D / /	Em / /	D / /	D / /
	She once	was a	true love of
	Then she'll	be a	true love of

Em / /	Em / /	Em / /	Em / /
mine.			
mine.			

▲ We are showing the first two verses of our arrangement of this traditional song.

▼ Your new chord Dsus. A 'sus' chord creates tension in the music.

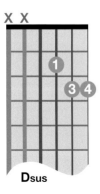

Dsus

X X

1
3 4

STARTING TO PICK

MUST KNOW

'Sus' Chords

Originating in medieval music, 'sus' chords create an elegant variation before a full major chord – in this case Dsus eventually moves on to D. Sus is short for 'Suspension', and describes a chord where the 3rd is raised up to a 4th (see pages 130-131), and if you want to hear a whole bunch of sus chords played one after the other, listen to the opening of The Who's Pinball Wizard.

Dsus

Cockles and mussels

The tragic story of Molly Malone: it seems Molly may really have existed in early 19th Century Dublin – and If you stroll down Grafton Street in Dublin you'll find a statue of her.

Track 30
How to play

Modifying patterns

Track 31
Play along

To extend the finger-picking technique a little further we are going to build on the previous pattern in which we played on two strings at a time. This time we are playing with the thumb and third finger at the beginning of the bar. On the 3rd beat, the third finger plays again, and in brackets there is an optional first finger picking on the 3rd string: if you feel that you are comfortable with the pattern you could try including this optional note – it will take a little concentration and a fair bit of practice before it is smooth. This is a great exercise in co-ordination. Remember: take it slowly and relax as you play.

▼ G, Em, Am, D⁷ and A⁷·

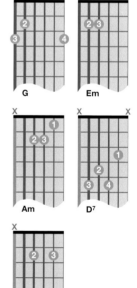

G   Em

Am   D⁷

A⁷

In the section 'Cockles and mussels alive, alive, oh!' you will see that for three bars in a row we have two beats of a G chord followed by just one of D⁷. As the D⁷ lasts for such a short amount of time, we need to create a special pattern just for that one beat, otherwise we will not be playing enough notes of that chord in the time allowed for it to be heard separately from the G chord. On the next page is a suggested pattern that incorporates the D⁷: you can see from this that there is a pick written for every

G / /	Em / /	Am / /	D⁷ / /
In Du - blin fair	City where the	girls are so	pre - tty I
Was a fish	mon - ger but	sure t'was no	won - der for
Died of a	fe - ver and	no - thing could	save her and

G / /	Em / /	A⁷ / /	D⁷ / /
First set my	eyes on sweet	Mo - lly Ma -	lone, as she
So were her	moth- er and	fath - er be	fore. They
That was the	end of sweet	Mo - lly Ma -	lone, but her

G / /	Em / /	Am / /	D⁷ / /
Wheels her wheel -	barr - ow through	streets broad and	narr - ow, crying
Wheeled their wheel-	barr - ow through	streets broad and	narr - ow, crying
Thyme.	barr - ow through	streets broad and	narr - ow, crying

G / D⁷	G / D⁷	G / D⁷	G / /
Cock – les and	muss-els a -	live, a - live	oh! A-
Cock – les and	muss-els a -	live, a - live	oh! A-
Cock – les and	muss-els a -	live, a - live	oh! A-

G / /	Em / /	Am / /	D⁷ / /
Live a - live	oh! A-	live a - live	oh! crying
Live a - live	oh! A-	live a - live	oh! crying
Live a - live	oh! A-	live a - live	oh! crying

G / D⁷	G / D⁷	G / D⁷	G / /
Cock – les and	muss-els a -	live, a - live	oh! (She)
Cock – les and	muss-els a -	live, a - live	oh! (She)
Cock – les and	muss-els a -	live, a - live	oh!

note of the D⁷ chord within a single beat, giving a full and bright sound. This is an example of where you might need to vary your normal picking pattern to accommodate new chords.

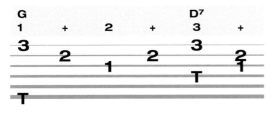

🎼 The melody for this song begins on a D – that's the open 4th string.

MUST KNOW

Pick'n'mix
Often you'll find the verse of a song can be picked and the chorus can be strummed, for instance, giving a more intimate feel to the verse and a more rousing effect for the chorus. You choose!

All through the night

Popularized by Peter, Paul and Mary in the 1960s, 'All Through The Night' is a lullaby, and – as Ar Hyd Y Nos – is one of the most popular of Welsh folk songs, beloved of male voice choirs.

Track 32
How to play

Track 33
Play along

Picking and strumming

In this song the chords generally change every two beats and in the third line they change every single beat! So you'll need a picking pattern that brings out the best of each chord in as short a time as possible, while allowing you to change smoothly and easily from one chord to the next. The following pattern repeats every two beats, so you can just keep going with it throughout the song - with one or two alterations where they are required. In the 4th bar, and again in the 8th bar and the 16th bar, the song remains on a single chord for four beats.

♪ The melody begins on a G – that's the 3rd fret of the top string, or the open 3rd string.

▼ All the chords in this song have appeared before.

G

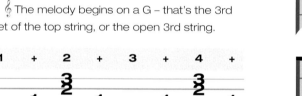

Alternating bass note

To avoid monotonous repetition of the pattern at these points, you could try picking an alternative bass note on the 3rd beat. You are playing a G chord, and the thumb would normally pick the 6th string. When you reach the 3rd beat pick the 4th string instead and listen to the way the new bass note adds variety. This technique – called *alternating bass* – is used extensively (see pages 66-67 for a fuller treatment).

Em

A⁷

G / Em /	A⁷ / D⁷ /	C / D⁷ /	G / / /
Sleep my love and	peace a - ttend thee,	all through the	night.
Ang - els watch-ing	ev -er round thee,	all through the	night.

G / Em /	A⁷ / D⁷ /	C / D⁷ /	G / / /
Guar - dian ang - els	God will lend thee,	all through the	night.
In my slum- bers	close sur- round thee	all through the	night.

Am G Am G	Am G Am G	Am G Am G	Am G Am D⁷
Soft the drow- sy	hours are cree - ping,	hill and vale in	slum-ber stee - ping,
They should of all	fears dis - arm thee,	no fore - bod - ings	should a - larm thee,

G / Em /	A⁷ / D⁷ /	C / D⁷ /	G / / /
I my lov - ing	vi - gil keep -ing,	all through the	night.
They will let no	per -il harm thee,	all through the	night.

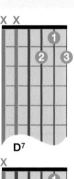

D⁷

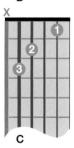

C

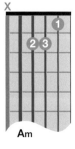

Am

As for the third line, why not return to a technique that you learnt earlier and simply strum down on each beat for each new chord: that way each new chord gets played instantly and you can concentrate on moving the left hand in time. The important thing is to play slowly enough to achieve a smooth and consistent performance.

Naming the patterns

Many of the patterns you are learning have evolved from classical pieces, ragtime, blues or folk and will be called different things by different people. For instance, the pattern on page 56 is known in some circles as the Three Finger Roll, or the Forward Roll, whereas T 3 2 1 is a Backward Roll. The order of fingers is a useful naming device: T 1 2 3 2 1 2 1, for instance. You might like to keep a notebook to write down strumming and picking patterns as you come across them, and build up a collection for reference – and of course name them as you see fit. Once you study alternating bass techniques (page 66) these patterns will really start to come alive.

Alternating bass patterns

An extremely easy way to create interest in your picking or strumming pattern is to alternate between two different notes in the bass. This gives the illusion of a separate bass line to accompany whatever is going on over the top of it. The rules for which notes to alternate are straightforward too.

Track 34
How to play

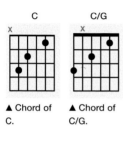

▲ Chord of C.

▲ Chord of C/G.

▲ With D7 you would alternate between the open 4th string (D) and the open 5th string (A)

▲ For Am you would alternate between open 5th string (A) and the open 6th string (E)

▶ Where T (for thumb) is followed by a small, raised 'a', this indicates an alternating bass note.

The root note of the chord is the one usually taken to be the bottom note. It is the note after which the chord is named. Look at the diagram on the far left. This is a chord of C. The lowest note of this chord is played on the 3rd fret of the 5th string, and is itself C.

The note to which this C bass note most readily alternates is the note that comes on the 5th degree of the scale: C - D - E - F - G.

The idea is always to find the root and fifth note of any chord and use them to alternate in the bass. And here's how it's done: if you are playing a 4-string or 5-string chord, alternate down to *one* string lower on the *same* fret: for C that was 5th string 3rd fret, to 6th string 3rd fret (see diagrams for more examples.).

Because we want to create a bass line, the idea is to find the lowest version for each note on the guitar. In the case of G, the lowest one is on the 3rd fret of the 6th string. Try playing this. What we now have is a C chord, but instead of a C in the bass we have a G. You would call this chord C/G (C with G in the bass). This would work nicely in the strumming pattern below. Don't forget to move the left-hand 3rd finger down to the 6th string for C/G.

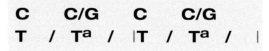

STARTING TO PICK

Moving the thumb

It would work equally well for a simple finger picking pattern: where you might originally play on a C chord, with the thumb always picking on the 5th string (see first diagram below)...

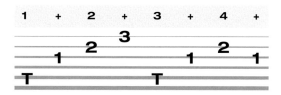

...you could try picking the second thumb stroke on the alternate bass note - in this case the G on the 6th string (see diagram below). Remember to move the 3rd finger of the left hand across to the 6th string for the alternating notes.

Always alternate between the normal bass note and the note on the same fret, one string lower. For a 6-string chord this clearly won't work because there is no 7th string to move down to!

Playing the E and G six-string chords

There are only two commonly played 6-string types - E and G. The rules here are simple:

For E chords (E, E7, Em, Em7 etc) alternate between the 6th string and the 5th string - you will be alternating between an E and a B (the 5th note of an E scale) in the bass.

For G chords (G, G7, etc) alternate between the 6th string and the open 4th string - you will be alternating between a G and a D (the 5th note of a G scale) in the bass.

B7

▲ B7 you would alternate between the 2nd fret of the 5th string (B) and the 2nd fret of the 6th string (F#) - in this case, as with C, you will need to move the left-hand finger to the new position (marked by an 'o') whenever you alternate the bass. Always alternate between the normal bass note and the note on the same fret, one string lower.

E

▲ For E chords alternate your picking thumb between the 6th string and the 5th string.

G

▲ In the case of the G chords, the 5th of the scale (D), is played on the open 4th sting. So alternate between the 6th string and the 4th string.

Careless love

Track 35
How to play

Track 36
Play along

One of the most popular and oldest of all American folk songs, Careless Love has been recorded by Janis Joplin, Bob Dylan, Johnny Cash and Elvis Presley.

Simple pick-strum pattern

The aim of this song is to get your fingers used to the idea of alternating bass. A simple pick-strum pattern might be best:

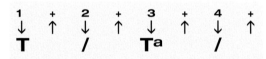

Once you feel comfortable with the basic pick-strum pattern you could try combining the alternating bass note with a standard picking pattern like the one below:

Alternating bass strings for each chord: C = 5 to 6; G⁷ = 6 to 4; C⁷ = 5 to 6; F = 4 to 5.

Alternating bass note rules

To recap the rules for alternating bass: on any chord that has its root on the 4th or 5th string, alternate between the normal bass note (the root) and the note one string lower on the same fret. For chords that have the root on the 6th string, you will either be playing an E-type chord or a G-type chord. For E, alternate 6 to 5, and for G alternate 6 to 4.

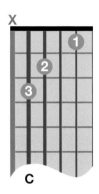

C

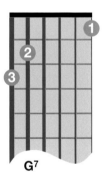

G⁷

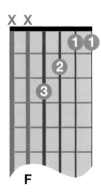

F

C / / /	G⁷ / /	C / / /	C / / /
Love, oh	love oh care - less	love.	
Once, I	wore my ap - ron	low.	
Now, I	wore my ap - ron	high.	

C / / /	C / / /	G⁷ / /	G⁷ / /
Love, oh	love oh care - less	love.	
Once, I	wore my ap - ron	low.	
Now, I	wear my ap - ron	high.	

C / / /	C⁷ / /	F / / /	F / / /
Love, oh	love oh	care - less	love.
Once, I	wore my	ap - ron	low, you'd
Now, I	wear my	ap - ron	high, you'll

C / / /	G⁷ / /	C / / /	C / / /
Look what	care-less love has	done.	
Fo - llow	me through rain and	snow.	
See my	door and pass it	by.	

Why not go back and look at some of the songs covered so far and try applying the alternating bass technique with the picking and strumming patterns you have learnt so far?

Incorporate the alternating bass style into your strumming and picking patterns, and you will soon find your sound has more depth, more variety, and, most importantly, more yee-hah!

Right-hand strum and pick

You are being asked to finger the chords with the left hand while strumming and picking with the right hand and at the same time thinking about alternating the bass with the left hand and maybe even singing along! That's a lot to do at once, so if you are finding it tricky, just try one thing at a time, maybe just picking the bass strings for each chord with the right thumb while fingering the shapes with the left hand.

🎶 This song begins with the note E – the open top string.

▶ # Banks of the Ohio

Banks of the Ohio is a great song for practising alternating bass. It was a hit for Olivia Newton John.

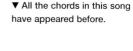

Track 37
How to play

Track 38
Play along

Different notes in the bass

This song and the previous one are designed to familiarize you with the idea of alternating the bass note. Having faithfully learnt which string is the bass note for each new chord, you now have to play different notes in the bass, and that might feel a bit strange at first. Take it slowly, and above all *listen* to what is happening in the bass. You'll soon get used to the sound and your ears will quickly become attuned to the bass line. The alternating bass technique is crucial for authentic picking and strumming styles.

As in the previous song, try a simple pick-strum pattern throughout the song to give you a feel for the alternating bass (as below).

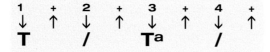

Once that is comfortable and you don't have to think too hard about it, you could try the following pattern:

I first came across this pattern (above) in a guitar piece called Silver Sand Rag and it would be suitable for any number of pieces of music, from Dylan's Don't Think Twice, and Simon and

▼ All the chords in this song have appeared before.

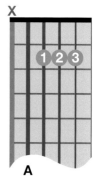

A

	A / / /	A / / /	E⁷/ / /	E⁷/ / /
I asked my	love,	to take a	walk.	To take a
(Chorus)	Say,	that you'll be	mine	in no-

E⁷ / / /	E⁷/ / /	A / / /	A / / /
Walk	just a little	walk.	Down be-
Oth	ers arms en	twine.	Down 'be-

A / / /	A⁷/ / /	D / / /	D / / /
Side	where the waters	flow,	Down by the
Side,	where the waters	flow!	Down by the -

A / / /	E⁷/ / /	A / / /	A / / /
Banks	of the O - hi -	o.	And on - ly
Banks	of the O - hi -	o.	And on - ly

Garfunkel's The Boxer, to classic ragtime pieces. It's not difficult providing you take it slowly at first and can play it in a relaxed, smooth fashion before you try playing it faster. Alternating bass strings for each chord: A = 5 to 6; E7 = 6 to 5; A7 = 5 to 6; D = 4 to 5. You should also make sure you are comfortable with each element before putting It all together.

Remember, playing slowly is great practise, because all the mistakes stick out a mile – playing fast can hide the mistakes but the overall effect can be shoddy and rushed.

♪ The melody for this song begins on an A, which is on the second fret of the third string.

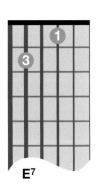

E⁷

X X

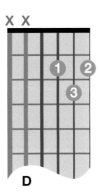

D

want to know **more?**

Take it to the next level...

Go to...
- ▶ **Start to Strum** – pages 42–51
- ▶ **Start to Pick** – pages 52–71
- ▶ **Using Bar Chords** – pages 72–91

Other sources
- ▶ **Guitar schools**
  attend regular evening classes
- ▶ **Music stores**
  for CDs, music magazines, local tuition, band forming and noticeboards
- ▶ **Internet**
  visit www.bangingsticks.com
  www.harmony-central.com/guitar
  www.guitargallerymusic.com
  www.actiontab.com for further guidance

using bar

chords

You've already come a long way since you first opened this book, and you are ready to tackle bar chords, which are played by reaching the first finger across all six strings. Bar chords are a stumbling block for some people, but accuracy, patience and practise will get you over this hurdle.

Bar chords explained

Certain chords are either tricky to play in the standard position, or else they sound thin. 'Barring' is a great alternative way to create new chords and is widely used in all guitar styles. It might feel strange at first but the key here is regular and accurate practise.

▲ If you play F without a bar, only four strings are used, and the lowest note (F) is sounded on the 3rd fret of the 4th string. This bass note isn't really low enough to make the chord sound full, so a bar chord is called for.

❶❷ Place the 1st finger straight across the strings, right behind the 1st fret wire. Then form a standard E shape in front of it with your other fingers: your bar chord is complete.

Using the E shape

We can harness the rich power of a big E chord to play F (and other chords). We'll go into the theory a little later, but for now all you need to know is that the note F is one fret higher than the note E.

Try playing the open 6th string (E), then the 1st fret on the 6th string (F) and you'll hear how close they are in pitch (the distance is called a semitone). If you were to raise every note in the E chord by one semitone you would be playing – hey presto – an F chord.

To play F as a bar chord place the first finger across all six strings on the first fret. Now form an E shape on the 2nd and 3rd frets. This effectively shortens the neck by one fret and so raises the pitch of the whole chord by a semitone. The resulting chord is a bigger, fuller, richer F than the 4-string version. With practice you will train and strengthen the muscles and develop the accuracy needed to hold the first finger in place.

❶   ❷

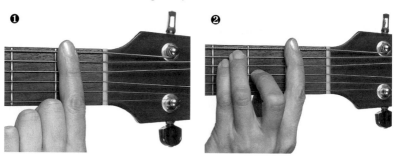

Using the A shape

Place the first finger across the 3rd fret, with the A shape on the 5th. When you play a standard A chord the shape is all on the 2nd fret, and we want to keep the same relationship between the shape and the end of the neck, so we'll leave a gap of one fret between your first finger and the chord shape. The resultant chord is an A in which every note has been raised by three frets, which will, in fact, give us a C chord. Try it, and then compare with the sound of a standard C shape. The notes will be in a slightly different order within the chord, but both C chords share the same basic sound.

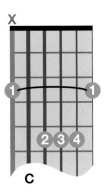

C

▲ This is the barred A shape creating a C chord in diagram form. You will come across this in further songs in this chapter.

◄ Now that you are playing a chord that derives from a 5-string shape, you will need to make sure that you are only strumming five strings - the bottom string Isn't played, because it isn't played in a standard A shape either.

MUST KNOW

How to achieve a well-balanced bar chord
- Always place the bar finger as straight as possible across all the strings.
- Keep the finger just behind the fret wire and you'll find you don't have to press it down so hard. It might feel uncomfortable at first but keep practising.
- The harder, outer edge of the finger should come into contact with the strings, not the fleshy underside.
- It might help if you bring the thumb slightly closer towards the body of the guitar, so the wrist naturally turns a little – this way the outer edge of the finger should be pressing on the strings.
- Before you form chord shapes with the other fingers, try moving the bar finger up and down the neck, placing it carefully in position each time. Now try plucking each string in turn to check the sound rings out and isn't dampened by the finger. In effect you are replicating a capo (see page 88).

Daisy, Daisy

Track 39
How to play

Track 40
Play along

It's time for bar chords! We are going to use the 6-string bar-chord F (see pages 74-75), an E shape barred on the 1st fret.

F bar chord

The F bar chord is based on an E shape.

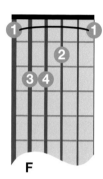

F

As discussed on pages 66-67, the alternating bass notes for an E chord are 6 to 5, so the same bass note alteration works for the 6-string F or any bar chord based on an E shape. Likewise, any bar chord based on an A-type shape will alternate 5 to 6.

Pick-strum-strum

The song has 3 beats, and you could play a simple pick-strum-strum pattern of the kind you played on Amazing Grace on pages 50-51. But this time, as each chord lasts for at least two bars, you could pick an alternating bass on every other bar. The alternating bass notes for each chord are as follows: C = 5 to 6; F = 6 to 5; G^7 = 6 to 4; D^7 = 4 to 5.

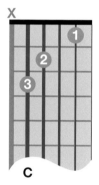

C

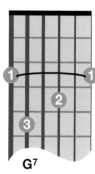

G^7

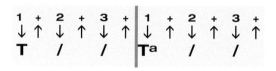

C / /	C / /	C / /	C / /
Dai -	sy,	Dai -	sy,

F / /	F / /	C / /	C / /
Give me your	an - swer	do	narr - ow, crying

| G⁷ / / | G⁷ / / | C / / | C / / |

G7 / /	G7 /	C / /	C / /
I'm	half	cra - -	zy,

D7 / /	D7 /	G7 / /	G7 /
All for the	love of	you.	It

G7 / /	G7 /	C / /	C / /
Won't be a	styl - ish	marriage,	

C / /	F /	C / /	C / /
Can't a -	fford the	carri - age,	But

C / /	G7 /	C / /	G7 /
You'll look	sweet u -	pon the	seat of a

C / /	G7 /	C / /	C / /
Bi - cy - cle	made	for two.	

Try changing smoothly from C to the bar-chord F and back to C several times without moving the 3rd finger of the left hand. The 3rd finger remains on the 3rd fret of the 5th string.

You have 4 bars of C before you need to change, so there's plenty of time to get ready. It might take some time to get used to playing bar chords so take it slowly: practise methodically over a few days and you'll see some progress.

A new version of D7 is introduced here: it's based on the C7 shape you learnt in Danny Boy. We're just moving it up a couple of frets to raise the pitch, so it now begins on a D. You can move the C7 shape up the neck to create new chords in the same way that you use bar chords. Be sure not to play the 6th or 1st (open) strings.

𝄞 The first note of the melody here is a G – top string, 1st fret.

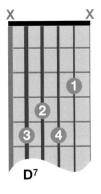

D⁷

Streets of Laredo

Track 41
How to play

Track 42
Play along

This old cowboy song was popularised by
Arlo Guthrie and was recorded by Johnny
Cash and Joan Baez. As with any old folk
song there are many versions around –
this is the version sung by Johnny Cash.

Quicker bar-chord changes

In this classic Western song, we are again going
to use the 6-string bar-chord F, and this time you
are required to change chords a little quicker.
Notice how the chord progression is almost the
same for every line of the song. Try to memorize
the chords of this song and you will find it easier
to concentrate on playing the song rather than
having to read it. Follow this simple up-and-down
finger-picking pattern.

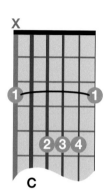

C

As you are picking, try varying the emphasis
slightly on each string as you go through the
pattern, and from one pattern to the next. This
will give your accompaniment a more 'textured'
feel, providing interest and variety.

We're now using an A-type bar chord for C:
remember to leave a gap of one fret between
the barre and the fingered frets. Practise
changing smoothly several times between C
and G⁷, as this is a common chord change so
it's worth learning.

🎼 This song begins with the note G – the 3rd
fret on the top string, or the open 3rd string
depending on your vocal range.

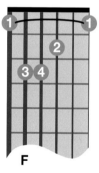

F

G⁷

C / /	F / /	C / /	G7 / /
As I walked	out on the	streets of La -	re - do, as
Six jo - lly	cow - boys to	ca - rry my	coff - in.

C / /	F / /	C / /	G7 / /
I walked	out on La -	re - do one	day, I
Six dance - hall	maid - ens to	bear up my	pall. Throw

C / /	F / /	C / /	G7 / /
Spied a poor	cow - boy wrapped	up in white	linen, wrapped
Bunches of	rose - s all	ov - er my	coff - in,

C / /	F / /	G7 /	C / /
Up in white	lin - en as	cold as the	clay. 'I can
Rose - s to	dead - en the	clods as they	fall. Then

C / /	F / /	C / /	G7 / /
See by your	out - fit that	you are a	cow - boy.' These
Beat the drum	slow - ly and	play the fife	low - ly,

C / /	F / /	C / /	G7 / /
Words he did	say as he	bold - ly walked	by. 'Come and
Play the Dead	March as you	carry me a -	long. Take me

C / /	F / /	C / /	G7 / /
Sit down be -	side me and	hear my sad	story, I'm
To the green	vall - ey and	lay the sod	o - er me,

C / /	F / /	G7 /	C / /
Shot in the	breast and I	know I must	die.' 'Get
I'm a young	cow - boy I	know I've done	wrong.'

MUST KNOW

Dominant-tonic relationship

G[7] and C are connected by what is known as the 'Dominant-Tonic Relationship'. What it means is this: if you listen to the chords that you are playing, you will hear that the song only sounds finished at the end of the fourth or eighth line. The rest of the lines end on a G[7], and this chord seems to hang in the air waiting to be grounded. It is the chord of C that grounds (or 'resolves') the G[7]. In fact, when you play the G[7] chord, the notes on the 2nd string (B) and 1st string (F) clash against each other in a dissonant sound – and it's the job of the C chord to resolve this dissonance).

Bar chord workout

Having understood the basic idea behind bar chords it's now time to extend this to include other shapes.

Variations on E and A

So far we have used two shapes to create bar chords: E and A. It is easy to use variations on these shapes to play pretty much any chord you like. For instance, if we return for a moment to the F bar chord on page 74, and bar this time not on the 1st fret but on the 3rd fret, the bottom note is no longer an F, but a G. (Compare with a standard G chord, and you will see that the bottom note of a G chord is on the 3rd fret of the bottom string.) In fact, you can bar and play this shape on any fret.

The diagram below Illustrates the names of the notes on the 5th and 6th strings. This way you can see at a glance where each note occurs on the bottom two strings, and you can position the barre accordingly.

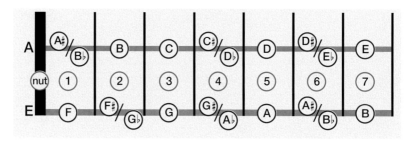

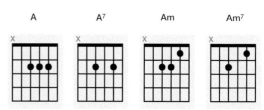

▶ These are the A-type shapes to use.

| E | E⁷ | Em | Em⁷ |

E E^7 Em Em^7

◀ These are the E-type shapes to use.

Use an A shape if you are following the notes on the 5th string, and use E shapes if you are following the notes on the 6th string. For example, if you wanted to play B^7, you could use an A^7 shape on the 2nd fret (B is on the 2nd fret of the A string) or you could use an E^7 shape on the 7th fret (B is on the 7th fret of the E string).

Remember to keep the bar finger nice and straight, and close behind the fret wire, with the hand turned slightly away to let the edge of the 1st finger press on the strings.

By the way: you might have noticed that we only moved up one fret to go from E to F, but need to move up two frets from F to G. If you are curious to know why, have a look at the theory section beginning on page 126.

Try to find the following bar chords using either A shapes or E shapes:

Bm, C⁷, F, Abm, Cm, Gm⁷, Bb⁷

You'll soon begin to memorize notes on the bottom two strings, and that will help you to find the right fret for your bar chords much more quickly. To begin with, try remembering that the 7th fret on the E string is a B, and that the 7th fret on the 5th string is an E.

Holding the finger in place

With practice you will train and strengthen the muscles needed to hold the finger in place. This is a slow process, and some people get frustrated with bar chords. Practise, and it will come right.

▼ Take your time, practise methodically, and have a little faith and you'll soon be wondering what all the fuss of bar chords was about.

Home on the range

Another great western song, recorded by
Gene Autrey, John Denver, Pete Seeger,
Neil Young, and – of course – Roy Rogers.

Track 43
How to play

Practising bar chords

Track 44
Play along

Pretty much every chord in this song will be
played with bar chords, so it's going to be more
important than ever to memorize the chord
progression so you can concentrate on the left-
hand positions. Try using just the first finger of
the left hand to begin with, playing the bottom
note of each chord as you whistle or hum the
melody. Take it slowly, and keep bashing away at
those bar chords. If it feels a little daunting right
now, why not revisit other songs we've played in
the book so far and play a few chords as bar
chords until you feel confident enough to tackle
this mammoth bar-chord work out.

▼ The barred chords giving
F, E^7, B♭, B♭m, G^7, C^7.

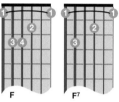

Playing C^7 unbarred and barred

For most of this song, it makes as much sense
to play C^7 the way you already know as it is easy
to change to and from the F bar chord. But
when you are coming from the new G7 bar
chord, you might like to try playing C^7 as a bar
chord as both the G^7 and C^7 are barred on the
3rd fret.

The song begins with the F that you played
on the previous two songs and if you remove
the 4th finger you'll be playing F^7 (E^7 shape
barred on the 1st fret). The B♭ is based on an A
shape, and the B♭m is based on an Am shape –
these are also barred on the 1st fret. The G^7 is
identical to the F^7, but is barred two frets higher,
on the 3rd fret, where the C^7 (based on an A^7
shape) is also barred.

▶ C7 as
you already
know it.

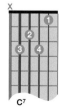

F / /	**F^7** / /	**B♭** / /	**B♭m** / /
Oh! ‖ give me a	home where the	buff - a - lo	roam, and the
F / /	**G^7** / /	**C^7** / /	**C^7** / /
Deer and the	an - te - lope	play.	Where
F / /	**F^7** / /	**B♭** / /	**B♭m** / /
Sel - dom is	heard a	dis - cou - raging	word, and the
F / /	**C^7** / /	**F** / /	**F** / /
Skies are not	cloud- y all	day.	

(Chorus)

F / /	**C^7** / /	**F** / /	**F** / /
Home,	Home on the	range,	where the
F / /	**G^7** / /	**C^7** / /	**C^7** / /
Deer and the	an - te - lope	play.	Where
F / /	**F^7** / /	**B♭** / /	**B♭m** / /
Sel - dom is	heard a	dis - cou - raging	word, and the
F / /	**C^7** / /	**F** / /	**F** / /
Skies are not	cloud- y all	day.	

Let's use a simple pick-strum-strum pattern again here so we can concentrate on the left hand. Remember – memorize chunks of the chord progression to enable you to focus on the left hand positions.

At the end of certain lines, you're playing the same chord for two bars. Why not put in some authentic Western alternating bass here? The F (being based on an E chord) alternates from the 6th string to the 5th string. C^7 (A^7 shape) alternates the other way: from the 5th to the 6th.

𝄞 The melody starts on a C, which is the 1st fret on the 2nd string.

1	+	2	+	3	+
↓	↑	↓	↑	↓	↑
T		**/**		**/**	

MUST KNOW

Chord coupling

There's a whole string of dominant-tonic chord moves here. F^7 wants to resolve to B♭, then in the next line there's a G^7 that – as you know – wants to lead to C. But instead of C there's a C^7, so the tension continues until it finally gets resolved: C^7 goes to F.

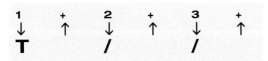

Greensleeves

Track 45
How to play

Track 46
Play along

**With lyrics said to be written by Henry VIII
and a melody possibly originating with a
Welsh lullaby, Greensleeves is probably
the best known of all early songs.**

Bar chords B⁷ and Bm

Compare the sound of the new B⁷ (an A⁷ shape
barred on the second fret) with the version of B⁷
you learned in 'John Brown's Body'. It's basically
the same sound, but this new shape can be
used anywhere on the neck to create any
'7' chord you need: just look at the diagram on
pages 80-81 to see which fret you need to bar
for the chord of your choice.

♪ Greensleeves begins on an E – the 2nd fret
of the 4th string.

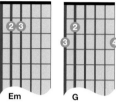

Em   G

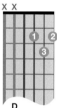

D

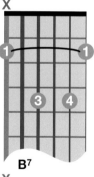

B⁷

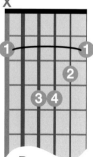

Bm

B⁷

Bm

Em / /	Em / /	D / /	D / /
A - las my	love you	do me	wrong to
Em / /	**Em** / /	**B⁷** / /	**B⁷** / /
Cast me	off dis -	court - eous -	ly; and
Em / /	**Em** / /	**D** / /	**Bm** / /
I have	loved you	oh so	long de -
Em / /	**B⁷** / /	**Em** / /	**Em** / /
Light - ing	in your	comp - a -	ny.
G / /	**G** / /	**D** / /	**D** / /
Green -	sleeves was	my de -	light,
Em / /	**C** / /	**B⁷** / /	**B⁷** / /
Green -	sleeves my	heart of	gold.
G / /	**G** / /	**D** / /	**Bm** / /
Green -	sleeves was my	heart of	joy, and
C / /	**B⁷** / /	**Esus** / /	**E** / /
Who but my	La - dy	Green -	sleeves.

The following pattern is a variation of the one for Scarborough Fair – with a twist. This time there is an alternating bass note on the 3rd beat.

▼ We also have a new sus chord: Esus. This is played by adding the 4th finger on the 2nd fret of the 3rd string.

Try to make the bass notes stand out in a regular, measured pattern at a fairly slow tempo.

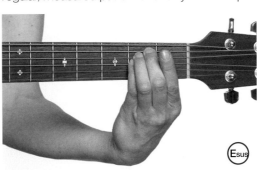

Esus

My grandfather's clock

This is the best known of many folk songs
Henry Clay Work wrote in the 1870s. It's
still a great favourite with children, and
has been recorded by Johnny Cash.

Track 47
How to play

Track 48
Play along

Bar-chord bonanza

Every chord in this song is a bar chord. But don't
panic, you could, of course, use the standard
chords for this song, and they are very simple –
so if you are struggling to make the bar chords
in time you could substitute a few for the chords
you already know. ideally, this song is a great
way to really nail those bar chords. The new G is
an E shape barred on the 3rd fret, whilst C is an
A shape also barred on the 3rd fret. D^7 is an A^7
shape barred on the 5th fret, and the A^7 is an E^7
shape also barred on the 5th fret.

   G and C are both barred on the 3rd fret: G as
an E shape, and C as an A shape. D^7 and A^7 are
both barred on the 5th fret: D^7 as an A^7 shape
and A^7 as an E^7 shape.

CHECK LIST

● Is your thumb sitting centrally on the back of
  the neck?
● Is the barre (bar) finger nice and straight, and
  parallel to the fret wire? And is it just behind the
  fret wire? Do you need to move your thumb
  slightly towards you to help turn the barre (bar)
  finger on its side?
● Can you hear all the strings ringing out clearly?
  Try plucking each string individually as you finger
  the chords to check how crisp the notes sound –
  are any left-hand fingers touching strings they
  ought to be avoiding?
● Take it slowly and smoothly; don't expect it to fall
  into place overnight, and you'll soon see progress.

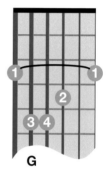

G

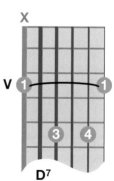

D^7

▲ D^7 is an A^7 shape barred
on the 5th fret (V= 5).

► The A^7 is an E^7 shape
also barred on the 5th fret
(V= 5).

G /	**D⁷** /	**G** /	**C** /
My Grand- father's	clock was too	large for the	shelf, so it
G /	**D⁷** /	**G** /	**D⁷** /
Stood nine -ty	years on the	floor.	It was
G /	**D⁷** /	**G** /	**C** /
Tall - er by	half than the	old man him -	self, though it
G /	**D⁷** /	**G** /	**G** /
Weighed not a	penn - y - weight	more.	It was
G /	**G** /	**C** /	**G** /
Bought on the	morn of the	day that he was	born, it was
G /	**A⁷** /	**D⁷** /	**D⁷** /
Al - ways his	trea - sure and	pride,	and it
G /	**D⁷** /	**G** /	**C** /
Stopped,	short,	never to go a -	gain when the
G /	**D⁷** /	**G** /	**G** /
Old	man	died.	

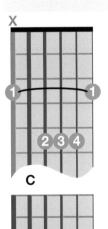

C

A⁷

There are only four chords in the song. Take It slowly and try to change smoothly. Accurate placing of the barre finger will help much more than brute force alone.

A 'tick-tock' effect

A simple strumming pattern might be helpful to let you concentrate on the left hand. You could just create a 'tick-tock' effect by plucking the bass note of the chord on the 1st beat and strumming down on the 2nd beat.

The melody begins on a D. That's the open 4th string.

Using a capo

The capo, or *capodastre*, is an invaluable device that takes the place of a barre. Stretched over any fret on the guitar neck, the capo effectively shortens the neck and changes the pitch of the chords being played.

Bar chords or a capo?

The difference between bar chords and using a capo is that the capo generally remains on a particular fret for the duration of the piece of music. So in some ways bar chords are more flexible, but in others the capo gives greater freedom because it frees up the first finger normally used for playing a bar chord and allows the player to use the first finger as normal; a capo can also 'barre' with any shape.

What is a capo?

Essentially the capo is a small clamp that fits over the guitar neck to shorten the vibrating length of the strings. They come in various styles, elastic or brass, and some with a straight face and some curved, depending on the profile of your guitar neck. Make sure you get some advice when you buy one from a guitar or music shop, and take your guitar with you to ensure a good fit.

▶ The two main styles of capo - the metal variety with rubber damper (near right) and the elasticated version (far right). Either capo is very simple to fit but you need to postion it firmly close to the fret to maintain a clear tone from the strings.

◀ Queen of American folk music Joan Baez uses a capo here to help raise the pitch of a song to a more comfortable key for her voice.

Playing with a capo

The chord shape (below left) produces the chord of C if played without a capo. By placing a capo on the 2nd fret (below centre), for example, the same shape now produces the chord of D. With a capo on the 5th fret the chord becomes F (below right). To play a whole tune (Early One Morning) using the capo, see page 90-91.

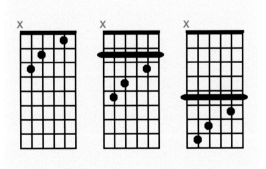

see page 90-91.

MUST KNOW

Raising the pitch

You can use a capo to raise the pitch of a tune so you can sing to a more comfortable key for your voice. If, for example, the capo were placed on the second fret, you would be raising the pitch of the song by one tone. So although you play a C shape on the first chord, it actually sounds like a D. The Am would sound like a Bm, and so on. See also pages 124-147.

USING BAR CHORDS

89

Early one morning

This story of jilted Mary is a favourite traditional English folk song. It's been recorded by Sarah Brightman, among others. The chords are very simple and the sequence is easy to remember.

Track 49
How to play

Track 50
Play along

Playing with a capo

This time the song has been written out with three different sets of chords – but you only play one set of shapes. The placement of the capo will determine the actual sound of the chord, so although the basic sound of the chord remains, its pitch has changed. Altering the pitch of an entire sequence of chords means that there is a change of key, and the process is known as *transposition*.

Try a simple picking pattern with this song – picking helps to bring out the delicate nature of the guitar when the capo is higher up the neck. As the tempo of the song is quite brisk it'll be enough to pick four times in the bar. The pattern below would do very nicely.

▼ Chords shapes below are shown without a capo. Placing a capo on the 2nd or 5th fret for C, for example, will produce the chord of D or F respectively.

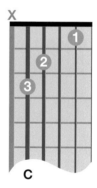

C

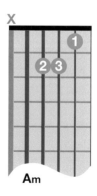

Am

USING BAR CHORDS

No capo	C / / /	Am / / /	Dm / / /	G7 / / /
2nd fret	D / / /	Bm / / /	Em / / /	A7 / / /
5th fret	F / / /	Dm / / /	Gm / / /	C7 / / /
	Ear - ly one	mor - ning just	as the sun was	ri - sing, I

C / / /	Am / / /	Dm / G7 /	C / / /
D / / /	Bm / / /	Em / A7 /	D / / /
F / / /	Dm / / /	Gm / C7 /	F / / /
Heard a maid- en	sing - ing in the	va - lley be -	low.

Dm / G7 /	C / / /	Dm / G7 /	C / / /
Em / A7 /	D / / /	Em / A7 /	D / / /
Gm / C7 /	F / / /	Gm / C7 /	F / / /
'Oh, don't de -	ceive me,	Oh, ne - ver	lea - ve me,

C / / /	F / / /	Dm / G7 /	C / / /
D / / /	G / / /	Em / A7 /	D / / /
F / / /	B♭ / / /	Gm / C7 /	F / / /
How could you	use a	poor maid- en	so?'

♪ The tune (starting on a D chord) begins on a D. That's the open 4th string. When you have two chords per bar, you might like to alter the pattern, otherwise some chords will barely be covered:

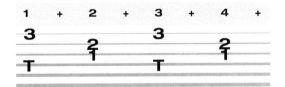

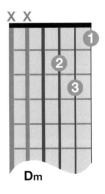

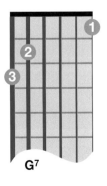

Dm   G7

want to know **more?**

Take it to the next level...

Go to...
▶ **Further techniques** – pages 92–10
▶ **Music notation** – pages 110–123
▶ **Music – in theory** – pages 124–147

Other sources
▶ **Your local music shop**
a great starting point for further study; become a regular and pick up tips and tricks from the helpful staff
▶ **Guitar lessons**
whether private lessons or group classes a weekly diary date will focus your study
▶ **Internet**
visit www.allmusic.com or www.cyberfret.com for all your needs

further

techniques

Once you've learnt the basic right-hand techniques of strumming and picking, and have a number of basic chord shapes to play in the left hand, it's time to explore some more sophisticated techniques commonly found in acoustic guitar styles. Whether folk, country or blues, these new techniques will help to give your playing an authentic feel.

Slap and Tickle

Tracks 51
How to play

Track 52
Play along

Until now we've looked at strumming patterns using up and down strokes with the thumb and fingers of the right hand. All manner of special effects can be achieved, however, by using the hand on the strings in different ways.

Fist and palm strokes

Let's begin with a rhythm technique that is widely used in strumming, in which the right hand is brought down on the strings to create a percussive sound. A related technique in flamenco guitar, known as the Golpe, uses the fingers to tap on the front of the guitar. Here you can either slap the hand down or make a fist, and the sound made will depend on a number of factors, including the force and point of impact.

To begin with, try bringing a fist down lightly onto the strings in a hand position similar to the one you use for strumming: just close up the hand a little for a loose fist, and make contact with the strings at the middle segment of the fingers, between the 2nd and 3rd knuckles. Here's a strumming pattern that brings out the percussive effect of the fist, creating either a silence (if you bring down the fist lightly enough) or some kind of knocking sound against the strings as it strikes.

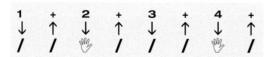

Remember to bring the hand down so that the thumb is in the correct place to begin the upstroke that follows. This means that when the hand lands on the 2nd beat, the thumb should be below the strings ready to begin the journey back up – otherwise you'll be making extra hand movements that are not only inefficient, but also mess up the rhythmic up-down-up-down movement at the heart of strumming.

If you'd like a more dramatic sound, try bringing the open hand down onto the strings, palm first, as though swatting a fly. Depending on your guitar, you'll most likely create a large, booming sound if you strike the strings right over the sound hole, and a more metallic, subtle sound if the impact is elsewhere. Either way you should aim for the hand to make contact on the strings with the thumb in a position to begin the following upstroke without any readjustment – this is an important point, so watch carefully that you're not making work for yourself.

Muting

Another commonly-used technique for the right hand involves plucking individual notes with the right thumb, but with the heel of the palm resting on the strings. The heel – the area at the end of the palm just before the wrist – should be gently pressed against the strings as close to the bridge as possible. The result is a woody, muted sound used in country, blues and rock music, often on electric guitars, and especially for bass lines. The palm against the string means that the string doesn't resonate as loudly or as long as it otherwise would. For a dirty rock sound, try strumming whole chords with the thumb this way, especially bar chords.

The example below is a typical blues *riff* strummed entirely with the thumb every half-beat, and with a simple chord in the left hand that changes with a movement of the left-hand little finger. Use the first finger to create the barre, and the little finger for the other notes. The underlined strokes in the diagram mean you should accent these strums a little more – and with an emphasis on the last half-beat of the bar, try bringing the first shape of the new bar forward to *anticipate* the first beat. The whole riff is played on the bottom three strings only.

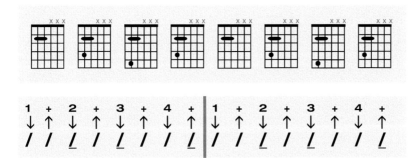

Mama don't allow

A great sing-along song, and a hit for
Hank Thompson, the 'King of Western
Swing'. Add other verses if you like:
among the things that Mama isn't keen
on include spinnin' around, foot stompin',
and bouncin' up and down – and of
course you could make up verses to suit
your own local matriarch.

Tracks 53
How to play

Track 54
Play along

Putting it together

This would be a great song to try out the hand
slapping/knocking technique we explored on the
previous page. The trick is precision: you'll need
to be sure that the hand slap or knock comes
down onto the belly of the guitar so that the
thumb lands below the strings, otherwise you'll
be making extra journeys with the strumming
hand and that will mess up the rhythm. Using the
strumming pattern below, you'll be playing down-
up-slap-up, down-up-slap-up throughout.

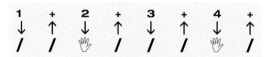

This song uses very standard chords, and you
could try playing the G and G7 as bar chords.
And remember the D7 from 'Daisy Daisy'? You
could use it here and, if you move your third
finger onto the 6th string, you could play
alternating bass: this chord is, after all, just a C7
shape a couple of frets higher. If you are playing
alternating bass here, you'll need to modify the
previous pattern slightly, so the thumb picks the
bass note on the 1st and 3rd beats, while the
hand still comes down on the 2nd and 4th beats.
It looks complicated, but it's more a case of

G / / /	G / / /	G / / /	G / / /
Mama don't allow no	guitar playing round	here.	
Mama don't allow no	hand clapping round	here.	

G / / /	G / / /	D⁷ / / /	D⁷ / / /
Mama don't allow no	guitar playing round	here.	
Mama don't allow no	hand clapping round	here.	Well

G / / /	G⁷ / / /	C / / /	C / / /
We don't care what	mama don't allow, we're	gonna play guitar,	any how
We don't care what	mama don't allow, we're	gonna clap hands,	any how

G / / /	D⁷ / / /	G / / /	G / / /
Mama don't allow no	guitar playing round	here.	
Mama don't allow no	hand clapping round	here.	

getting used to the pattern. Learn this one and you'll certainly be set for the barn dance!

🎼 The first note of the melody is G, the open 3rd string.

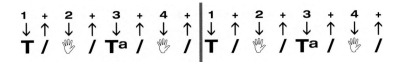

◀ Peter Rowan with his bluegrass background has helped fuel the acoustic music revival for nearly 40 years. Born in Boston 1942, he worked with, among others, Bill Monroe, one of the giants of country music and father of the bluegrass style, and Tex-Mex accordionist Flaco Jimenez.

The Irish washerwoman

Being a jig – a type of dance popular in Ireland from the 16th Century – this melody was originally composed without any lyrics, although over the years several versions have subsequently been penned, often with humorous political content.

Tracks 55
How to play

Track 56
Play along

Strumming triplets

A jig is a dance with two beats to the bar but – unlike a two-beat march or quickstep – the jig beat splits into 3, so there are six subdivisions to the bar. A beat divided into three is known as a 'triplet'. You can read more about time signatures in the theory chapter, where you'll see mention of 6/8 and an excerpt from the notation for this tune.

Here are the bare bones of the jig rhythm. You'll see that the beat is now divided not into two, but into three. Try counting '*one*-and-a *two*-and-a' as you go, and notice how, when you reach the second beat, it is played with an upstroke. This might feel strange at first, but – as always – try it slowly and calmly to begin with, working up the pace when you feel comfortable.

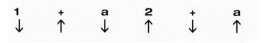

◄ With standard strumming, the 2nd beat is played with an upstroke.

Alternatively, you could emphasise the 2nd beat with a downbeat – this way you are playing two down strokes together, with no upstroke in between. This method is sometimes used by guitarists playing the jig rhythm, but the fact that the pattern of up-down up-down is disturbed means that the hand has to make a quick and unnecessary move up between the two down strokes.

<table>
<tr><td>‖G /</td><td>|G /</td><td>| Am /</td><td>| Am /</td><td>|G /</td><td>|G /</td><td>|D /</td><td>|G /</td><td>|</td></tr>
<tr><td>|G /</td><td>|G /</td><td>| Am /</td><td>| Am /</td><td>|G /</td><td>|G /</td><td>|D /</td><td>|G /</td><td>‖</td></tr>
<tr><td>|G /</td><td>|G /</td><td>|D /</td><td>|D /</td><td>|C G</td><td>|C G</td><td>|D /</td><td>|D G</td><td>|</td></tr>
<tr><td>|G /</td><td>|G /</td><td>|D /</td><td>|D /</td><td>|C G</td><td>|C G</td><td>|D /</td><td>|D G</td><td>‖</td></tr>
</table>

1	+	a	2	+	a
↓	↑	↓	↓	↑	↓

◄ An alternative pattern, with the 2nd beat now played with a downstroke.

With six parts to the rhythm, the obvious subdivisions are either two beats of three (1 + a 2 + a), as above, or three beats of two (1 + 2 + 3 +), as with Amazing Grace or Home on the Range. Try alternating between the two different rhythms by changing the emphasis. Rhythm guitarists playing in this style often slip in a couple of bars of the three-beat rhythm to add variety and excitement:

▼ Try alternating the first rhythm here with the second, every few bars, for an unpredictable and exciting sound.

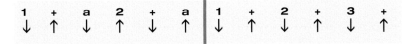

1	+	a	2	+	a	1	+	2	+	3	+
↓	↑	↓	↑	↓	↑	↓	↑	↓	↑	↓	↑

Now try these strumming techniques for yourself: this tune goes at quite a lick, so loosen your belt, warm up your wrists, and release the hand brake!

In the second half of the tune, you are asked to change between C and G quite quickly. Place the fourth finger on the 3rd fret of the top string on the C chord, and leave it there for G – this should speed the change up considerably.

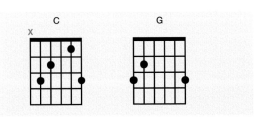

◄ Place the fourth finger on the top string ready for the G chord to make the change between the two smoother.

Hammer-on and pull-off

A great trick for embellishing finger picking, in bass lines or chords, is the 'hammer-on'. Used with care, you'll be able to create rich and interesting picking patterns for many styles.

Hammer-on explained

Have a look at the example below. At the beginning of the bar, you are fingering a standard C chord with the left hand – except that the 2nd finger is missing from the 4th string. On the first beat, pick the bass note (5th string) with the thumb, and pick the 4th string on the next half beat. Now comes the interesting part: the second finger is placed onto the 4th string on the 2nd fret (the usual position for a C chord) with enough force to make the string sound. The second finger literally hammers onto the 4th string, without any right-hand picking. This is known as the hammer-on, and is used extensively in rock, blues, country, jazz – some of the hammer-ons you'll find yourself doing fit so nicely under the fingers that it's not hard to see why they have found their way so abundantly into guitar technique.

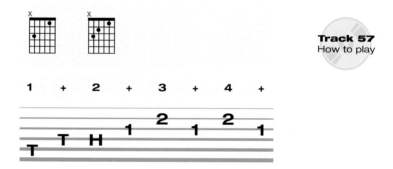

Track 57
How to play

FURTHER TECHNIQUES

Here's another example, again on a standard C chord. This time the picking pattern is embellished by a hammer-on towards the end of the bar: on the fourth beat, the thumb picks the open 4th string, and the left-hand second finger quickly comes down to play the hammer-on. All this happens before the last half-beat of the bar, when the first finger plays the third string. So here the hammer-on happens within a 16th of a bar. Have a listen to the CD example if it's not clear, but either way you should try it at a nice relaxed tempo first. And again, the sound is made without any right-hand picking, created instead entirely by the impact of the left-hand finger coming down quickly onto the string.

Pull-off

The companion technique for the hammer-on is known as the pull-off. In this technique a finger that is already on the fingerboard pulls away by dragging over the string, picking the string in the process. Here's an example:

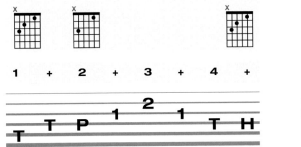

Track 59
How to play

This time, you are starting with a standard C shape, picking the bass note (5th string) with the thumb. The thumb goes on to pick the 4th string on the next half-beat. On the 2nd beat, the left-hand second finger is taken away, but it picks the 4th string as it does so – pull the finger in towards the palm, and you should hear the finger pick the string. On the 4th beat, the 4th string is still open, so pick it with the thumb again and hammer back on with the 2nd finger on the last half-beat of the bar.

Practise these techniques slowly and methodically, and go through the various chords that you've learnt one by one: you'll see that certain hammer-ons and pull-offs lend themselves especially well to particular chords. Often, the hammer-on begins with an open string that gets filled by the normal finger for the chord, as in the above examples. But you could experiment further: the following G chord, for instance, could have a simple hammer-on onto the 5th string, but you could add a note to the chord by hammering on to the 4th string, or 2nd string – try the examples below to add some variety to your standard chord shapes.

FURTHER TECHNIQUES

101

Waltzing Matilda

Track 60
How to play

Track 61
Play along

**The unofficial National Anthem of Australia,
written by 'Banjo' Patterson. It tells the story
of a roving 'swagman' (hobo) who poaches
a jumbuck (sheep) and avoids capture by
the squatter (land-owner) by jumping into
a billabong (water hole). His ghost invites
us to 'Waltz Matilda': to wander through the
landscape with your bedroll. So now you know.**

Complex picking patterns

Now we're going to pull together two separate
elements studied in this chapter. Firstly, this song
is written with two beats in the bar, but as with
the Irish Washerwoman, those beats are
subdivided into three, so it contains two triplets in
each bar. Secondly, the loping rhythm of this
piece lends itself well to a picking style with
hammer-ons, so we'll throw that into the mix.
The two triplets make the music roll nicely along –
try humming 'Teddy Bear's Picnic' for a few bars
to get the feel of the rhythm.

Here's a suggested picking pattern with a
hammer-on in the second beat where the thumb
plays the open 5th sting which is immediately
fretted by the 2nd finger of the left hand. This
diagram is for G:

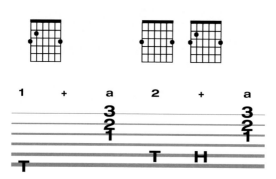

◀ You'll begin with a full G
chord but on the 2nd beat
the 5th string is open, and
is hammered on
immediately afterwards by
the left-hand 2nd finger. The
three fingers play together
on the last pick of each beat.

G /	D /	Em /	C /	G /	Em /	C /	D /
Once a jolly	swagman	camped by a	billabong,	under the	shade of a	coolabah	tree and he

G /	D /	Em /	C /	G /	C /	D /	G /
Sang as he	watched and	waited til his	billy boiled	Who'll come a-	waltzing Ma-	til - da with	me'.

G /	G /	C /	D /	G /	C /	G /	D /
Waltzing Ma-	til - da	Waltzing Ma-	til - da	Who'll come a-	waltzing Ma-	til - da with	me',and he

G /	D /	Em /	C /	G /	C /	D /	G /
Sang as he	watched and	waited til his	billy boiled	Who'll come a-	waltzing Ma-	til - da with	me'.

Of course when you change chord the hammer on will change too. There are four chords in this song, and all but D have lower string notes that are easy to hammer on, as shown below.

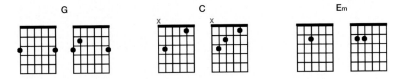

Hammer-ons and pull-offs can be combined in quick succession. Here below is an example of an embellishment for the D chord. Play the regular picking pattern in the first half of the bar, then on the second beat hammer-on with the little finger on the top string. Pull the little finger off again on the next part of the beat, making sure it plucks the top string as it goes, and on the last part of the beat pull off with the usual top string finger (which might be either your first or third finger, depending on the way you play this chord) – again letting it pluck the top string. You'll notice I've also put an alternating bass note in on second beat. This pattern is tricky! Try looping this exercise round several times to get it smooth.

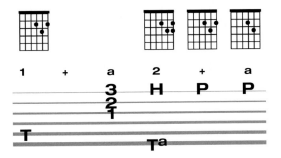

Bass runs in bluegrass

Once you have your alternating bass smooth and automatic, it's time to customize it with some added notes to liven up the bass line.

Bluegrass picking

In bluegrass picking this is a major feature and gives your accompaniment an authentic feel. Let's look at a couple of examples. In the first example there are two bars of G7, followed by C, and you would normally alternate the bass 6th to 4th on the G7 chord, with 5th to 6th on the C chord, using a simple pick-strum pick-strum pattern:

G⁷ / / / |G⁷ / / / |C / / / |C / / / |

T / Tᵃ / T / Tᵃ / T / Tᵃ / T / Tᵃ /

A common feature of bass picking is to provide a little extra interest by climbing up or down from one bass note to another using *passing notes*. Guitarists calculate (and many of them do it on the spot) how many beats are needed to climb up or down. On the 1st beat of the 2nd bar, the bass note is a G, then there are another 3 beats before you are asked to play a C at the beginning of the 3rd bar. Between these two notes are found two others: A and B. A is the open 5th string, and B is the 2nd fret on the 5th string. Two extra notes in the bass means two extra beats for bass picking, and these will take place on the 3rd and 4th beats of the 2nd bar. So let's look more closely at the 2nd bar: on the first beat, you'll pick as normal, on the 6th string; on the second beat, strum as normal; on the third beat, picking the open 5th string (remove the 2nd finger in the left hand); on the fourth beat

> **WATCH OUT!**
>
> **Notation**
> All these diagrams are a little unwieldy – but of course that's why we have guitar notation, which we'll be studying in the next chapter!

FURTHER TECHNIQUES

replace the 2nd left hand finger and pick the 2nd fret of the 5th string. On the first beat of the next bar you'll land on a C, on the 3rd fret of the 5th string, and you will have climbed systematically up from G to C:

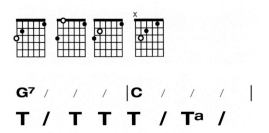

G⁷ / / / |C / / / |
T / T T T / Tᵃ /

◀ A *scalar* run that goes step-wise along part of the scale – in this case from G – through the passing notes A and B – to C.

Track 62
How to play

In the theory chapter you'll learn much more about scales and intervals: this will allow you to make your own bass runs that fit perfectly in the key of the song and in the rhythm of the beat.

Here's another suggestion for the same passage – this time with a single passing note that comes right at the end of the bar, taking the place of the last strum of the second bar. You will play the alternating bass note (D on the open 4th string) for G7 on the 3rd beat, then play the note that comes between D and C: C#. This is found on the 4th fret of the 5th string.

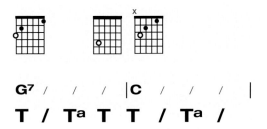

G⁷ / / / |C / / / |
T / Tᵃ T T / Tᵃ /

◀ Another passing-note, this time moving down a fret at a time – this makes it a *chromatic* passage.

Track 63
How to play

Sweet baby's arms

A song made famous by Lester Flatt & Earl
Scruggs, the unlikely-named but very
popular bluegrass duo. This song has also
been recorded by Tammy Wynette &
George Jones, and Buck Owens, to name
a few, but my favourite is the great version
by Bill Monroe, the father of Bluegrass. A
great one to get everyone singing along.

Track 64
How to play

Track 65
Play along

Customized picking

Now it's time to try a few of the tips and tricks from this chapter. Hammer
on bass notes, pull 'em off again, and use a smattering of *scalar* or
chromatic passing notes. Here's a pattern for the chord of G using new
strings for the alternating bass line. Up 'til now we've been alternating
between the root note and the note on the next string down (except for 6-
string shapes where we've modified the technique). Now we'll pick the
bass on various strings. Try the pattern below:

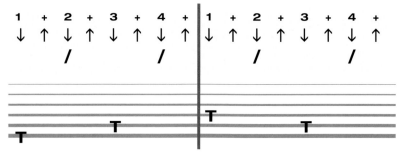

You could even hammer on, on the 3rd beat of each bar. Begin with the
open 5th string, quickly bringing the 2nd finger down onto the 2nd fret.

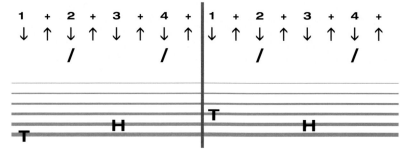

G / / /	**G** / / /	**G** / / /	**G** / / /
Roll - in' in my	sweet ba - by's	arms,	
Where were you	last Fri - day	night,	
Ain't gonna	work on the	rail road,	

G / / /	**G** / / /	**D⁷** / / /	**D⁷** / / /
Roll - in' in my	sweet ba - by's	arms,	
While I was	layin' here in	jail?	You were
Ain't gonna	work on the	farm.	Gonn-a

(Row 1 col 4: Gonn-a)

G / / /	**G⁷** / / /	**C** / / /	**C** / / /
Lay a - round the	shack 'til the	mail train comes	back
Walk - in' the	streets with an -	other	man
Lay a - round the	shack 'til the	mail train comes	back

G / / /	**D⁷** / / /	**G** / / /	**G** / / /
Roll - in' in my	sweet ba - by's	arms,	
Wouldn't ev - en	go my	bail.	Well I
Roll - in' in my	sweet ba - by's	arms,	

Typical bass run

For variety, try picking the following notes on the last 3 beats of the very last bar to lead into the next verse. Don't do it every time as it could get monotonous, but this an idea of the sort of variety you could add with practice.

𝄞 The first note of this song is G, the open 3rd string.

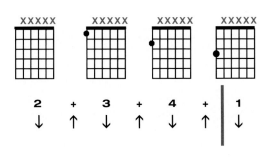

◄ Starting from the second beat of the bar, and moving up a fret at a time from the open 6th string, you'll eventually land on the 3rd fret at the beginning of the next bar – chromatically rising to the bass note G at the start of the new verse. Listen to these chromatic passing bass notes on the CD.

She'll be coming ...

This is the best known of all American mountain songs and you'll notice that it has identical chords to Rollin' in my Sweet Baby's Arms. This is a very common chord progression and the feel here is the same as the previous song.

Track 66
How to play

Track 67
Play along

More patterns

Here's a pattern for the chord of G, similar to the one in the previous song. Now it's been developed a little in the second half. You are asked to hammer on to the 4th string (the 2nd fret will do nicely) at the beginning of the second bar, and to pick the 4th string (open) and 5th string (2nd fret) on the last two beats. Try using this as a variation of the earlier example, and add your own variations.

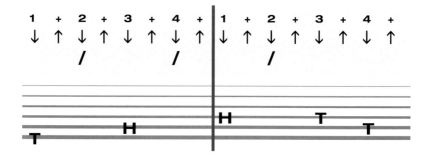

Why not try sketching out your own picking patterns on paper? In the next chapter you'll learn tablature, a system of notation designed just for the guitar that makes it really easy to jot down ideas on paper so you don't forget them.

In this style of music the bass line is extremely important, and you now have a number of techniques at your disposal. First, memorize a simple Alternating bass version for this chord sequence, then perhaps substitute one or two of the bass notes for hammer-ons, or else place a smattering of hammer-ons on other beats. Finally string together the bass notes, particularly targeting the bass note at the beginning of the bar, with passages of scalar or chromatic passing notes.

	G / / /	G / / /	G / / /	G / / /
She'll be	coming round the	mountain when she	comes.	- She'll be
	Pulling six white	horses when she	comes.	- She'll be
	Wearing pink py -	ja - mas when she	comes.	- She'll be

G / / /	G / / /	D⁷ / / /	D⁷ / / /
Coming round the	moun-tain when she	comes.	She'll be
Pulling six white	horses when she	comes.	She'll be
Wear-ing pink py -	jamas when she	comes.	She'll be

G / / /	G⁷ / / /	C / / /	C / / /
Coming round the	moun-tain.	coming round the	mountain, she'll be
Pulling six white	horses.	pulling six white	horses, she'll be
Wear-ing pink py -	jamas.	wearing pink py -	jamas, she'll be

G / / /	D⁷ / / /	G / / /	G / / /
Coming round the	moun-tain when she	comes.	She'll be
Pulling six white	horses when she	comes.	She'll be
Wear-ing pink py -	jamas when she	comes.	

For further variety, try playing this song with the capo on the guitar neck – you choose the fret. Although the chord shapes will be the same, the song will 'feel' different at a different pitch and might give you a different perspective on some of the sounds you are making. And, as with any of these songs, you might find the music is in a range that is easier for you to sing. Don't forget to revisit these simple songs once you've worked through the Theory chapter, as you'll then have the skills to transpose the songs into any key you like.

♪ The first note of the melody for this song is D, the open 4th string.

want to know more?

Take it to the next level...

Go to...
- ▶ **Start to Strum** – pages 42–51
- ▶ **Start to Pick** – pages 52–71
- ▶ **Using Bar Chords** – pages 72–91

Other sources
- ▶ **Your local guitar/music shop**
  for your favourite artists' guitar playing books and other music scores and books
- ▶ **Guitar schools**
  attend regular evening classes or go for private one-to-one tuition
- ▶ **Internet**
  visit www.supersonic.net/guitar
  www.guitarlessonworld.com and
  www.guitarnoise.com

music

notation

Sooner or later you are going to want to write down some of your musical ideas, or at least play other peoples'. Notation and – for the guitar – tablature, are both great ways to write down musical information and, as we shall see, it's not at all difficult to learn. So let's get started.

How to read music

Music notation is a simple system for recording what note should be played when. It can also give an indication of expression - how softly or loudly (the dynamics), or how slowly or fast (the tempo), or how smoothly or detached (the articulation) the music should be. Many musicians use notation to jot down ideas they have for melodies or for exercises to practise, and many more read notation from the hundreds of song books on sale.

The basic staff

Let's begin by looking at the way different notes are displayed. All notes appear on a 5-line grid known as a staff (or stave), and are placed on a line or in a space between lines. Each line or space has its own note name, and the lower the note appears on the staff, the lower its pitch. In the diagram below you can see where each note belongs.

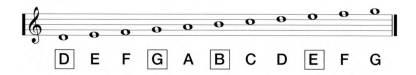

D E F G A B C D E F G

The guitar has quite a low voice and the bottom two strings appear well below the staff. Here are all six guitar strings notated.

▲ Notice the boxed letters – these are the top four guitar strings.

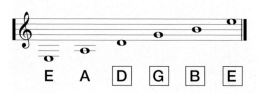

E A D G B E

◄ Here they are again with the bottom two strings. Notice, too, the extra leger lines. Leger lines extend the range of the staff (or stave) – the grid for placing music.

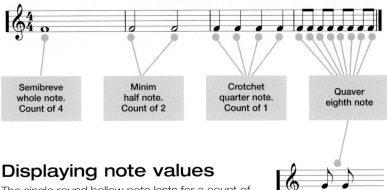

| Semibreve whole note. Count of 4 | Minim half note. Count of 2 | Crotchet quarter note. Count of 1 | Quaver eighth note |

Displaying note values

The single round hollow note lasts for a count of four, and is called a whole note, or semibreve. The hollow note with a stem (the vertical stalk) lasts for a count of two, and is called a half note, or minim.

The black note with a stem lasts for a count of one, and is called a quarter note, or crotchet.

The black note with a stem and flag (the horizontal beam) is called an eighth note, or quaver. If a quaver appears on its own, it looks like this:

Sometimes, of course, the music might want to show a rest – that is, a place where there is no note. As all the rhythm symbols in a bar need to add up to the number of beats indicated by the time signature, it is sometimes necessary to include symbols that show silence.

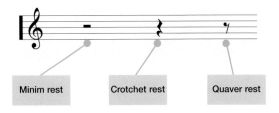

| Minim rest | Crotchet rest | Quaver rest |

The clef

That squiggle sitting at the beginning of the staff is a G clef (nicknamed 'treble' since it is used by high-sounding instruments such as the violin, the saxophone, or the guitar). Instruments with a lower range, such as the bass guitar, or the trombone use a different symbol: the F or bass clef.

Dotted notes

Sometimes it might be necessary to include note-lengths that can't be shown with the symbols we already have. A dot following a note increases its time value by half. In the example below the first note is now worth one and a half beats. Look at the minim at the end of the first bar – it is tied to the first crotchet in the second bar. It is one continuous note, with the value of a dotted minim (three beats) – but there isn't enough room left in the first bar for a note worth three beats, so it flows over into the second bar.

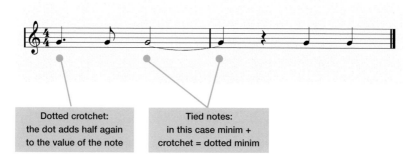

Dotted crotchet:
the dot adds half again
to the value of the note

Tied notes:
in this case minim +
crotchet = dotted minim

MUST KNOW

Other time signatures

Another very common time signature is 3/4: Amazing Grace, or Home On The Range, for instance, have this time signature. It is possible, however, to use other note values to represent a beat. The time signature of 6/8, for example, is often used for an Irish Jig, and has 6 quavers in the bar in two groups of 3. (Think of the 'diddely-diddely' rhythm of the Irish Washerwoman to get the 6/8 time signature).

Time signatures

The numbers that appears at the beginning of a piece of music are time signatures, and tell us two things: the top note shows how many beats there are in a bar and the bottom number shows what kind of note is used to represent one beat. The example (see diagram on page 113) is in 4/4, which means that there are four beats in the bar, and each beat is represented by one crotchet – which is why you have two minims in the bar, for instance, or eight quavers.

Sharps and flats

You'll notice that we use seven different letter names for the notes, A, B, C, D, E, F and G – but often these notes are either raised or lowered slightly in pitch. For this the following symbols are used: A sharp (♯) raises the note by one fret on the guitar, and a flat (♭) lowers the note by one fret. Therefore if you were to play a D (third fret, second string), the next note up the neck on the same string would be a D sharp – D♯. But if you lowered the D by one fret you would be playing a D flat – D♭.

You'll learn much more about sharps and flats in the theory chapter that follows. For now all you need to know is that sharpening a note means raising it by a fret, and flattening a note means lowering it by a fret.

▼ 4/4 is such a common time signature that it is sometimes displayed as 'common' time. This is represented by a '𝄴' at the beginning of the music.

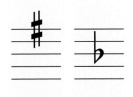

▲ A sharp (left) raises a note by one fret. A flat (right) lowers a note by one fret.

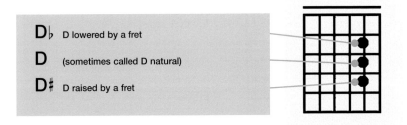

D♭   D lowered by a fret

D   (sometimes called D natural)

D♯   D raised by a fret

Repeats

To save space, sections that are repeated in the music are often only written once – but appear within brackets called repeat marks. Repeat marks always appear in pairs, as this example shows:

Repeat from here...

... to here

We'll also come across a few other symbols in the notated music starting on page 120. In the meantime, here's a chart showing the names of the notes on the first few frets of the guitar neck. See if you can use this chart to play the piece of music in the diagram on page 115. Recognize it?

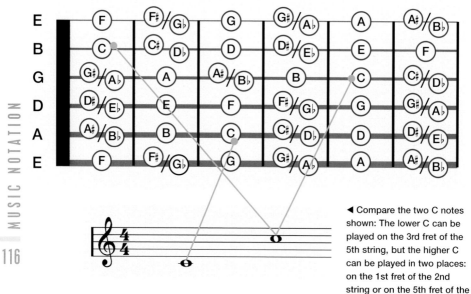

◀ Compare the two C notes shown: The lower C can be played on the 3rd fret of the 5th string, but the higher C can be played in two places: on the 1st fret of the 2nd string or on the 5th fret of the 3rd string. Many notes can be found in more than one place.

Guitar tablature

We've seen how notation can be used to display note durations, pitches and rhythms. Now we're going to take a look at another form of notation designed especially for guitar music: tablature. Often referred to as 'tab', this notation can be used on its own or in conjunction with conventional notation to give all the information needed.

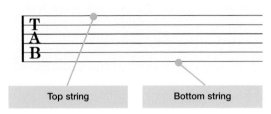

Top string

Bottom string

◄ Here's an empty tablature staff. Instead of the 5-line staff we saw before, this one has 6: one line for each string. The notes on the bottom string are represented by notation on the bottom line, and the top string by the top line.

In tablature, numbers are entered to correspond to the fret number that should be played on each string. In the example below the first note, C, is played on the 3rd fret of the 5th string. Later in the bar a G is played with the open 3rd string.

Numbers refer to the fret on which the note should be fingered

You might see tablature with note-stems: this system gives an indication of the duration of a note (which you don't get with standard tablature) but is less common than the previous example:

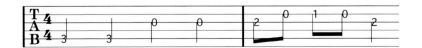

Study no. 1 in G

Track 68
How to play

Now it's time to put into practice the information on notation that you've been wading through. The following short piece of music is notated by both conventional and tablature systems of notation.

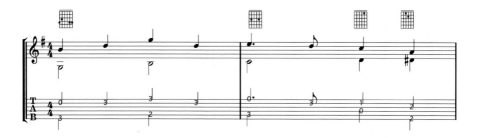

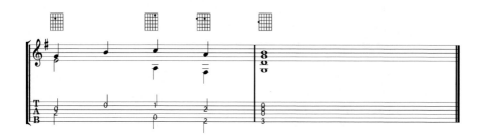

Following the dots

Take a look at the beginning of the top staff and you'll see a sharp (#) symbol resting on the top line – the F line. This indicates that every time an F is displayed it should be played as an F#. In fact, in this piece, there is only one F, at the end of the second bar. It should be played as F#, on the second fret of the bottom string. Music often contains either sharp or flat symbols at the beginning to tell you whether any of the notes are sharpened or flattened. This is known as the key signature, and is discussed in detail in the theory chapter beginning on page 126.

At the end of the second bar the D is played as a D#: this is a temporary alteration to the pitch of the note, known as an *accidental*.

You'll also notice that chord shapes are included above the top staff – these are actually for your guidance and don't represent complete chords, but they suggest a fingering position at various places in the piece.

Finger positions

As a general rule you could keep the right-hand fingers on the usual strings (1st finger on the 3rd string, 2nd finger on the 2nd string and 3rd finger on the 1st string) but you might often find it easier to alternate between the 1st and 2nd fingers if you have a fast sequence to play: this is what classical guitarists would do.

It might be necessary to move one or more left-hand fingers as you go through the music. The second note in bar 2, for instance (D quaver) should be played by placing the 4th finger on the 3rd fret of the 2nd string, but you might find it easier to wait until you are ready to play the D rather than placing the 4th finger in position at the beginning of the bar.

On the 4th beat of the 3rd bar, you are asked to play an A and an F#, for which you will need your 3rd finger on the 3rd string and your 2nd finger on the 6th string – and although you could place them in position on the 3rd beat, you might find it easier to wait until the previous notes have been plucked, using the 3rd beat to prepare your fingers for the 4th beat.

If you get stuck with the top staff (conventional notation), cross-refer it with the bottom staff that has guitar tablature. Remember that the tablature tells you what fret each note should be played on. You might find it useful to clap the rhythm through, remembering to count all the time, until you are familiar with it.

Tails up and tails down
In standard notation, notes above the middle line have tails pointing down, and notes below the middle line point up – this is just a case of keeping things tidy. In guitar music, however, notes with the tails up are played with the fingers and those with the tails down are played by the thumb.

MUSIC NOTATION

Study no. 2 in Am

Track 69
How to play

Here's another little piece to practise. This time you are asked to play standard shapes that you'll recognize. Once you have familiarized yourself with the picking pattern you'll see that the pattern repeats, more or less, for every bar.

Memorizing

Try memorizing the chord progression: Am, Dm, G⁷, C, Am, Dm, E⁷, Am. Now memorize the picking pattern and the piece will pretty much play itself.

New symbols

Some other symbols are included here: take a look at the first bar and you'll see the letters 'mp'. This stands for *mezzopiano*, an Italian term meaning moderately soft. The letter 'p' is used for *piano* (soft), 'f' for *forte* (loud), and 'm' for *mezzo* which is Italian for 'half' (or moderately). You are asked to play the music moderately softly to begin with but by bar 4 you should be playing loudly (*forte*). You'll notice that these dynamic markings are connected by a long hairpin-shaped symbol. This is a *crescendo* marking and simply means that you should gradually get louder, rather than suddenly getting louder at bar 4. In the second half of the piece, you'll see that you are asked to gradually get quieter, this time with a *diminuendo*, until you finish at the same quiet level with which you started.

Another new symbol appears over the last note – an arc with a dot below it. This is a pause symbol, and simply means that the note or notes that appear under it should be held a little longer than usual. It's often found at the end of a piece.

MUST KNOW

Dynamics

p (piano) and *f* (forte) can be used to indicate varying degrees of volume. *pp*, or even *ppp* can indicate very quiet passages, through *p* to *mp*, *mf*, *f*, and *ff* or even *fff*. The French Romantic composer Hector Berlioz wrote something silly like *fffff* sometimes, but then he was a little over-the-top. And ever so loud.

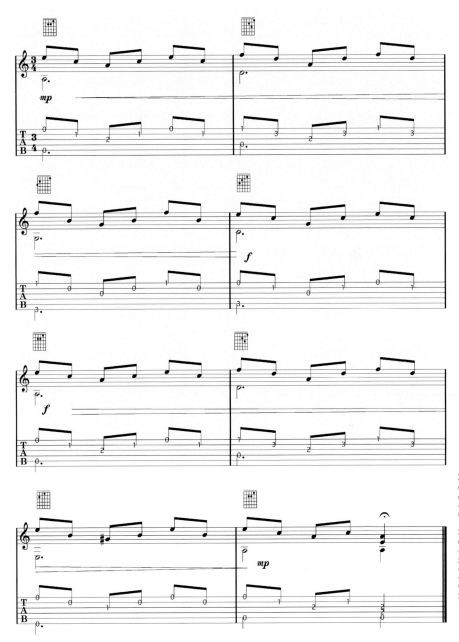

Gingernut Rag

Track 70
How to play

**Now for something completely different... a third and final
notated piece of music, and this time it's in the style of a rag.**

Syncopation

In the first and second bars the melody hangs on the end of the second beat while the bass note changes. This is a typical ragtime and jazz sound, known as syncopation. Syncopated music includes off-beat melody notes played over a steady beat. Try emphasizing the C in bar two for that authentic sound. If you like the style, listen to Stefan Grossman or the old ragtime guitarists like Rev. Gary Davis and Mississippi John Hurt.

The most important characteristic of a ragtime piece is that the quavers are 'swung'. That is to say that the quavers are not exactly half a beat apart: the first quaver is slightly longer, and the second quaver a little shorter to create a jazzy rhythm (think of the 'Raa-ta Taa-ta Ta' in Manhattan Transfer's 'Chanson d'Amour'). You'll also notice that the thumb plays an alternating bass pattern on the 1st and 3rd beats of the bar, and you should try to keep the bass beat constant.

This is quite a difficult piece – it needs careful preparation and practice. Don't skimp over the bits that are giving you trouble – go back over them again and again until they are polished. Pay careful attention to which left-hand fingers are needed, and go logically through from one chord to the next to find the most efficient way to change. And as with all pieces of music the sense of satisfaction is proportionate to the amount of work you put in. To me, going through a difficult piece over and over until it's finally nailed is a great feeling, and I reckon if you can play this piece through smoothly you will be beaming with pride!

◀ The squiggles just before the A⁷ chord in bar 6 and the C chord in bar 8 are symbols for strums – you are asked to strum down across the notated strings with your thumb. Be careful not to confuse them with the crotchet rests that appear between the bass notes!

want to know more?

Take it to the next level...

Go to...
▶ **Music – in theory–** pages 124–147
▶ **A world of styles –** pages 148–173

Other sources
▶ **Your local music shop**
   for further study of music books, music scores, and plenty of guitar songbooks
▶ **Guitar lessons**
   whether private lessons or group classes a weekly diary date will focus your study
▶ **Internet**
   www.dolmetsch.com/musictheory1.htm
   www.musictheory.net and
   www.emusictheory.com

music —

in theory

In case you're wondering how or why these chords all fit together the way they do, and how you might put them together in a composition of your own, we are now going to peer into the world of triads, tritones, semitones, and tonics. Then we'll take a look at improvising techniques for rock and blues guitar, and how to write your own sequences.

The major scale

Track 71
How to play

As a musician you'll want to know something about the way notes, scales and chords work. You have already learnt a fair amount of theory just by working through the previous chapters. Now it's time to consolidate what you've already learnt and to delve a little deeper into the world of music theory.

Tones and semitones

The smallest distance of pitch in Western music is called a semitone. That's the distance between any note on the guitar and the note one fret higher or lower – frets divide the neck into semitones. Take another look at the fingerboard chart on page 116 to see how the notes are arranged on the neck. If you move two frets up or down you are covering a distance of two semitones, known as a tone. If you go up 12 semitones (6 tones), you'll arrive at a note that has the same name as the note you started with – you have covered an interval of an octave: the distance between C on the 5th string and C on the 2nd string, for instance. We tend to use particular combinations of notes to build melodies and chords, and these combinations of notes exist together in a scale.

▼ The notes below represent a scale of C. If you play it on the guitar, you'll notice that the distance between each note is not always the same. Although the distance (or 'interval', as it's known) is usually one tone (two frets), at certain places in the scale the interval is half the size: a semitone.

Tone interval (T)

Semitone interval (S)

T T S T T T S

C D E F G A B C

The shape of scales

The sequence of intervals in the scale of C is
T-T-S-T-T-T-S. This sequence gives a particular
characteristic to the scale, and it is known as a
major scale. This scale, then, is the scale of C
major.

Start on a different note and follow the same
sequence of intervals T-T-S-T-T-T-S, and you'll
still be playing a major scale. The following
example shows a scale of G major.

MUST KNOW

Shorthand
T-T-S-T-T-T-S is short
for Tone-Tone-
Semitone-Tone-Tone-
Tone-Semitone.

This time, you'll notice, there's a sharp – F#. The
reason for this is simply that if there were an F
natural (not sharp) in the seventh position, the
sequence of intervals would no longer make a
major scale (remember – there's only a semitone
between E & F, so in this case the F is raised a
semitone to F#). So In G major, an F# is used.
Take a look at another example, a major scale
starting on F:

With the F major scale, the B becomes B♭ –
again to preserve the Tone-Tone-Semitone-
Tone-Tone-Tone-Semitone (T-T-S-T-T-T-S)
sequence. You can start a major scale on any
note (there are 12 different ones altogether) and
each time you will end up with a different
number of sharp or flats.

Remember, a scale is simply a selection of
notes over a range of an octave that can be
used together.

MUST KNOW

The scale
The word scale
comes from the Italian
'scala' meaning
ladder. Notice the
rising shape of the
major scale.

Key signatures

In music notation a number of sharps or flats is placed at the beginning of the piece to show which key the music is in – how many sharps or flats are used. This is known as the key signature.

Here is a diagram showing all the key signatures, starting with one sharp and one flat. If, for example, you wanted to play a scale of A major, or to play a melody in the key of A major, you would need to make sure all the F's, C's and G's were sharp (#). And if you wanted to play in E♭ major, you would need to play B♭ wherever a B is written, and an E♭ when an E appears.

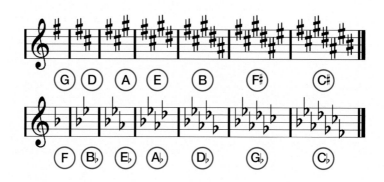

On page 133 you'll find a very useful diagram known as the Circle of Fifths that displays all the keys in a logical order. Every key has a different key signature: common keys on the guitar include G, D, A, E and B♭ – and, of course, the key with no sharps or flats, C.

MUST KNOW

Major and minor
Melodies built from notes of a major scale tend to sound bold and bright: Cockles and Mussels is in a major key. On page 136 you'll learn about minor scales, which sound dark and mournful: Greensleeves is in a minor key.

All about chords

Chords are made by combining notes from a scale starting at the bottom and selecting every alternate note: the first, third and fifth notes of the scale.

The chord of C

Let's look at an example in the key of C: The triad is made of the root (C), third (E) and fifth (G).

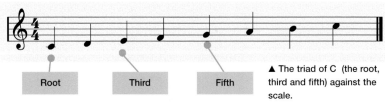

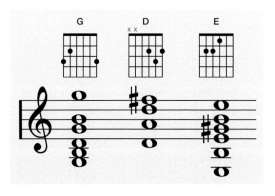

▲ The triad of C (the root, third and fifth) against the scale.

The first note of the scale (known as the 'root')- combines with the third and fifth notes (referred to from here on as the 'third' and 'fifth' of the chord) of the scale to make a chord of C. When you play a C chord on the guitar you are, in fact, playing a combination of Cs, Es and Gs. In fact in this case you are playing C, E, and G, and then another C and E in the next octave.

This method of building triads and chords works for any key. Just take the root, third and fifth of a scale to build the basic chord for that key. Here are another few examples:

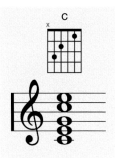

▲ Chord shape for C showing which notes of the C scale are used.

◄ Chord shapes for G, D and E showing which notes are used.

Triads

Of course, you could use any combination of the root, third and fifth – the combinations that are played in these common chord shapes just happen to be 'handy' on the guitar. If you play bar chords, for instance, you'll be playing the same notes but in another order.

You can use the notes of a scale to build more than one chord - by playing alternate notes from your starting point you can create chords on any note of the scale. These groups of three notes are known as *triads*. Because the notes of the scale are not equally spaced, the chords made by these triads don't all sound the same. Here are the triads for C major:

Track 72
How to play

▼ The triads in the key of C, showing which chords are made.

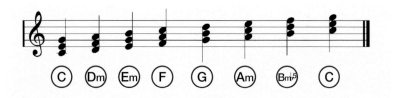

The notes make a range of different major and minor chords. The major chords are the ones in which there is an interval of four semitones between the root and the third (the bottom two notes of the chord). This interval is known as a *major 3rd*. The minor chords have an interval of three semitones between the bottom two notes, known as a *minor 3rd*.

The seventh triad is a little complicated to use and is generally avoided: it has its uses but doesn't come up too often, so for now we'll concentrate on the first six chords of the key.

These chords can be combined to make chord sequences: for most of the songs you have played in this book the majority of the chords have been taken from a single key.

MUST KNOW

Roman numerals
Chords are traditionally numbered with Roman numerals: one is I, two is II, three is III, four is IV, five is V, and six is VI. You'll find this method of numbering used in most books.

Diatonic chords

Here are the diatonic (meaning belonging to a specific scale) chords for some other keys:

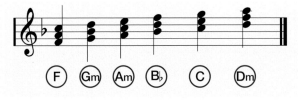

F   Gm   Am   B♭   C   Dm

◀ The triads of F major. Notice how the order of major and minor is exactly the same as in C major.

G   Am   Bm   C   D   Em

◀ Here are the G major triads - again, the same pattern of chords.

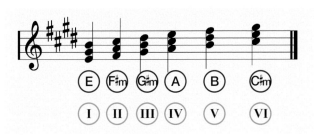

E   F#m   G#m   A   B   C#m

I   II   III   IV   V   VI

◀ And the E major triads this time showing the Roman numerals (I-VI). A great shorthand for understanding harmonies.

Common triads

On close examination of the above diagrams, you will see many of the same triads appearing in different keys. For example, C appears in the top diagram as the fifth triad (**V**) in the key of F and the fourth triad (**IV**), in the middle diagram, in the key of G.

Hopefully through studying these diagrams you'll have started to see a pattern emerge. In any major key, the first, fourth and fifth (**I**, **IV**, **V**) chords are major, and the second, third and sixth (**II**, **III**, **VI**) chords are minor. If you are putting together a chord sequence for a new song, or trying to work out a song from a recording, these are the most likely chords to be used.

MUST KNOW

Three-chord trick
You might have heard the expression 'three-chord trick' – it's used to describe a song that uses the first, fourth and fifth chords in a key. Many people, from Bob Dylan to Status Quo, have written songs that only use these three chords.

Four-note chords

So far we've concentrated on three-note chords (triads). Interesting harmonies occur when we add a fourth note.

Here are the triads of C again, but now with another note added – the seventh.

▼ The 4-note chords for C major.

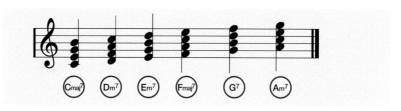

Try these shapes to hear the characteristics of the three types of chords we now have. Each chord has a particular 'flavour', or character. Listen to Cmaj^7 (**I**): it has a floaty, calm quality about it, whereas G^7 (**V**) sounds somehow restless or anxious – as though it wants to move on to another chord. Am^7 (**VI**) is not so different from Am, a little darker and warmer perhaps.

Track 73
How to play

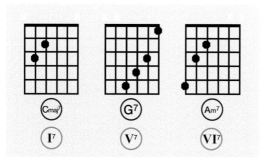

Dominant-tonic relationship

The difference between Cmaj^7 and G^7 is especially interesting. In song 3, and again in songs 17 and 18, the Dominant-tonic relationship was mentioned, and now it's time to explore it a little more. Chord **V**^{7} (the *Dominant*) always wants to go to chord **I** (the *Tonic*): the 3rd and

7th of G⁷ are separated by an interval that is exactly half an octave, known as a tritone. This interval is actually very dissonant (the two notes clash) – the best way of resolving this dissonance is to move on to C.

The 7th of G⁷ is crucial to the overall sound of the chord – but the 7th of a maj⁷ chord, like Cmaj⁷ and Fmaj⁷ here, is just an embellishment of the original sound. That's why it's important to include the 7th in a V^7 but not necessarily in I or IV. By the way, if you want to know how to play the maj⁷ chords (also written as Δ) on the guitar, check out the shapes in the Jazz Styles section starting on page 170.

Chord V with a 7th (V^7) has an extremely important role to play: it helps to move the music along, and provides movement in the chords. Without V^7, chord progressions would sound very bland. Revisit any of the songs you've played in the book so far to hear how crucial V is in creating interest, suspense, movement, tension and general musical energy.

Circle of fifths

Now that you understand the way V^7 moves to I, you might like to take a look at the following diagram.

It's known as the Circle of fifths (some people call it the *Cycle* of fifths) because it shows how V^7 moves to I. Start from any note, and if it's a V^7, I will be one step anti-clockwise around. D⁷, for instance, goes to G. Ab⁷ goes to Db. B⁷ goes to E. Of course, if you want to know what V^7 is and you already have I, move clockwise one step. You can clearly see that if you keep going you'll eventually come back to the chord with which you started.

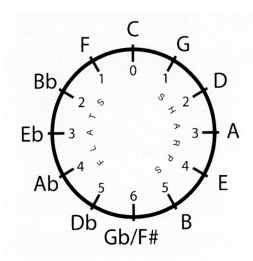

◀ Another great use for this diagram is to show the number of either sharps or flats needed in a key signature: compare this diagram with the one on page 128 and see how convenient the Circle of fifths is. Notice how the letter names F, B, E, A, D, and G are repeated as you move around the circle making it easier to memorize, and that keys opposite each other are pitched a tritone apart: D to Ab, for example, or F to B.

Your own music

You will doubtless want to consolidate this theory with some practical exercises, and you'll certainly want to put all this new-found knowledge to good use, so it's time to start writing your own progressions.

You might be sceptical at first but when you see how straightforward it can be, you'll be putting pencil to paper and coming up with your compositions that are every bit as good as songs you hear every day on the radio.

A glance back over the songs studied in this book will show you that they all have one thing in common: structure. Pretty much every song is built in 4 or 8-bar blocks that work in pairs. This basic form is universal in folk, pop, rock, jazz and any popular genre. So begin by marking out an empty 8-bar block on a sheet of paper (as shown below).

| (Bar 1) | (Bar 2) | (Bar 3) | (Bar 4) |
| (Bar 5) | (Bar 6) | (Bar 7) | (Bar 8) |

Choose a key and fill the bars

Now let's decide on a key – G major will do for starters. You know that in any major key chords **I**, **IV** and **V** are major, and **II**, **III** and **VI** are minor. In the key of G this makes G, C, and D, and Am, Bm and Em. You also know that **V** should be **V**^{7} for it to function as the dominant chord, so D becomes D^7. Therefore G, Am, Bm, C, D^7 and Em are the chords we will use to create this piece of music. Now it's time to start putting the chords in. We'll start and end with the tonic G (**I**), so put that in at bars 1 and 8. And, if you're going to end on **I** you'll probably want **V**^{7} before it, so put in D^7 at bar 7.

Making music

You're left with 5 bars to fill – they don't have to be filled with one chord per bar, you could have more chords, or fewer, but a chord per bar is a good medium choice for now. The rest is up to you. Think about the mood of the piece, whether you want to put a few gloomier minor chords together, or whether you want some sunnier major chords, or perhaps a bit of both. You might be strumming your guitar as you put the chords together, and perhaps humming a tune that you're beginning to hear.

Alternatively, you might just want to fill the chords in at random before you hear a note. And when it's done you might want to tinker with it a little, or add another 8 bars (possibly in a different key), or write some lyrics. However you do it, when it's done, it's yours. You wrote it, and with just a few simple rules.

A little sophistication

Now look more closely at some of the songs in the book. Remember how in Home on the Range the chords moved from B♭ to B♭m? That's **IV** moving to **IV**m, a common device for a more sophisticated sound: the equivalent of C to Cm in the key of G. And in the same song, where C^7 was chord **V**, C^7 was approached by the dominant of C: G^7. So G^7 went to C, which itself turned out to be the dominant of F. G^7 was 'piggybacked' onto C^7 – again, this is a very common device. The dominant of the dominant is used to heighten the tension and to delay the resolution. And it has a great name: '*secondary dominant*'. In fact *any* chord in a key can be approached by its own dominant chord in the same way.

Below is an example of a chord progression in another key put together using the simple ideas discussed in this section, together with a break-down of the devices used.

IVm to follow IV. Don't over-do this one, but it can be effective

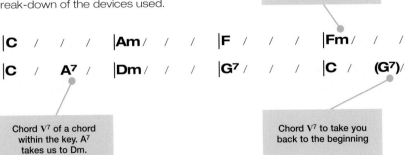

|C / / / |Am / / / |F / / / |Fm / / / |

|C / A^7 / |Dm / / / |G^7 / / / |C / (G^7)/ ‖

Chord **V**^{7} of a chord within the key. A^7 takes us to Dm.

Chord **V**^{7} to take you back to the beginning

𝄞 This example is in the key of C.

Minor scales

Major scales and keys create 'happy' upbeat music. We use minor scales and keys to create a huge variety of moods. On these pages we explore the key of E minor.

When using the notes of a major scale it generally follows that the music wants to come to rest on the tonic note (the note after which the scale is named). However, it is possible to construct melodies that seem convincingly to come to rest on another note of the scale. The opening of the melody for Scarborough Fair, for example, uses the notes of the G scale, yet you can clearly hear that the music wants to land and rest on an E:

Track 75
How to play

Are   you   going   to   Scar – bo – rough   Fair

This piece of music uses the notes of a G scale but the melody is structured in such a way that the ear hears E as the tonic note – and the melody has a mournful quality. In fact what is happening here is that another key, a minor key, is being created from the notes of the G scale. We are hearing the relative minor key of G: E minor.

The relative minor occurs on the 6th degree of a major scale. In G the relative minor is E minor – here's the E minor scale.

▼ The scale of E minor, the relative minor of G major: this version is known as the *natural* minor.

Play the scale over a few times and you will hear how, despite using the same notes as G major, this scale has a darker, wistful quality.

A potential problem can occur when using this scale to create melodies: as the E minor and G major scales use identical notes, it's all too easy for the melody to want to 'slip' back into G major. To avoid any confusion, an alteration is often made to the scale: the seventh is sharpened to create an interval of a semitone at the top of the scale, just like in a major scale. This helps to distinguish E as the tonic:

▼ A minor, this time with a sharpened seventh. This version is called the *harmonic* minor.

The harmonic minor scale is used a great deal, and never runs the risk of being mistaken for G major. However, the interval between the 6th and 7th notes in the scale is now 3 semitones wide, and for many purposes this is simply unwieldy and unmelodic. For this reason a further alteration is often made. The 6th is also sharpened to even out the intervals at the top of the scale:

▼ E minor, now with a sharpened 6th and 7th. This version is known as the *melodic* minor.

On page 143 you'll find fingering diagrams for various minor scales.

MUST KNOW

Modes

It is actually possible to make any note of a major scale sound as though it is the tonic note through careful structuring of the melody and some supporting harmonies. These scales-within-keys are known as *modes*. The mode we used to build the minor scale (major scale starting on the 6th mode) is known as the *aeolian* mode, and is the most common. Building a mode starting on the second note of a major scale (the *dorian* mode) is also widely used in jazz and folk.

Other scales

Many different kinds of scales occur in folk music, and some of these have found their way into jazz, rock and blues guitar.

Pentatonic scale

The most important of these is the pentatonic scale. In fact, the pentatonic scale is found in virtually every music culture in the world. The biggest pitfall in using a major scale to build a melody over a given chord is that the major scale contains certain notes that are only a semitone from chord tones, and these notes can cause dissonant clashes between the melody and the chord. By removing potentially troublesome notes the scale becomes 'foolproof' – any note within it can be used to play over the tonic chord with no risk of clashes.

Essentially the pentatonic scale (so called because it contains five notes) is a major scale with these 'clash-able' notes removed. Take a look at the C major scale (below) and you'll see that two notes are only a semitone away from chord tones: the fourth (F), which is a semitone from the third (E); and the seventh (B) which is a semitone below the tonic (C).

MUST KNOW

The 6th
Although A isn't actually the 6th note of C pentatonic it is called the 6th because it is the 6th note of the C major scale – and the major scale is the ultimate point of reference. For the same reason the E in the A minor pentatonic is known as the 5th: In A major E is the fifth note.

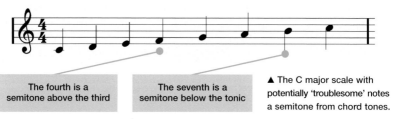

The fourth is a semitone above the third

The seventh is a semitone below the tonic

▲ The C major scale with potentially 'troublesome' notes a semitone from chord tones.

Removing the 4th and 7th leaves five notes – the pentatonic scale:

▼ C pentatonic scale.

Listen to the melody of Amazing Grace or Swing Low, or the verse of Oh, Susannah (CD tracks 22, 24 and 8): they are all built entirely from a simple pentatonic scale. Many of the greatest folksongs and hymns use only notes from a pentatonic scale. In folk, rock, and blues, it's common to use this scale with a slide up to the 3rd, to create a more vocal, or smoother, sounding scale. This is achieved by including the note one fret below the 3rd – in this case an E♭.

Track 76
How to play

▼ Pentatonic scale with a flattened 3rd.

Try playing notes from the pentatonic scale, and approach the 3rd by playing the flattened 3rd before it and sliding your left finger up a fret to the natural 3rd. You'll find the scale takes on a warm, lyrical quality.

Track 77
How to play

Blues scale

Remember the relative minor? It uses the same notes as a major scale but begins on the 6th. Well relative minor pentatonic scales are very popular. Instead of starting the C pentatonic scale on C, start it on A (and don't forget to include the flattened 3rd – which now becomes the flattened 5th of the new scale).

▼ A minor pentatonic scale with a flattened 5th, more commonly known as the blues scale. Try the blues scale for a great lead guitar sound.

This scale is so well-used in rock and blues that it is more commonly known as the blues scale. You'll find fingering charts for these scales on the following pages.

Track 78
How to play

Blues improvisation

Once you have mastered chord shapes, strumming and picking, you'll want to have a go at playing lead guitar.

Playing lead guitar

Over the next few pages we'll look at various scales you can play on the guitar, and ways in which they can be used to play lead. Playing lead is really about improvising melodies over a chord progression. The great guitarists make it look easy – because it is! Over the next few pages you'll pick up scales and tips that might not turn you into BB King or Eric Clapton overnight, but they will send you on your way.

The great thing about the scales that you learn is that you can play them anywhere you like on the neck. Here are two versions of the blues scale, one starting on A and the other on G. Try to keep a separate finger for each fret of the scale: the first finger should remain on the starting fret, the second finger on the next fret up, the third finger on the next and the fourth finger on the last fret in each shape. This means you will actually only use the fourth finger on the sixth and second strings – and the first finger plays the slide on the second string, whereas the third finger plays the slide on the fifth string, because then you'll end up with the finger in the right position and you will have preserved the fingering pattern for the shape:

▼ A blues (top) and G blues (bottom). Notice how they are identical except for the starting position.
-Ⓞ- indicates the root note of the scale.
━◖━ means 'slide' from this note up to the next note.

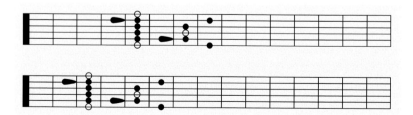

Scale patterns

This pattern stretches over two octaves – so the root note of the chord is played three times. Have a look at the A blues scale and you'll find a low A played on the 6th string, a middle A played on the 4th string, and a high A played on the top (1st) string.

You could easily memorize this scale in terms of the number of the finger used. On the bottom string you use the first finger and then the fourth finger; on the fifth string you use the first finger and then the third, and so on. So you could express this scale as 1-4, 1-3, 1-3, 1-3, 1-4, 1-3, remembering the slides, too. Many people think of scale patterns on the guitar in this way.

Of course, the standard major pentatonic is often played, too – here's C pentatonic. You'll notice that it's almost identical to the A blues scale, except that it starts and ends on C – A blues and C pentatonic are really two versions of the same thing.

▼ C pentatonic, a variation of A blues. These two scales have the same relationship as the relative major and minor scales discussed on page 136.

When do you use these scales?

Later in this chapter you'll find some specific chord progressions over which you could try playing notes from these scales in melodic, improvised lines. For now you should investigate the character of the different scales, and how the notes within them interact with each other. One of the best ways to do this is to learn some 'licks'. These are phrases that soloists have come up with over the years, and which are included in other soloists' improvisations. Every lead guitarist has an arsenal of licks at his or her disposal.

Track 79
How to play

Learning some 'licks'

Below are illustrated a few well-known rock and blues licks that will help you to get a feel for what pentatonic and blues scales can do. Below is a G blues lick: you can play the D♭ (the flattened 5th) by fingering as shown, or bend the string with your finger on the 5th fret to sharpen the C by a semitone, then straighten the string for the C.

A lick in C (below), using the pentatonic scale with the flattened 5th. Great for swing and boogie styles, or a B B King-style blues sound. Slide from the 6th fret to the 7th fret for a smooth move from the D# (flattened 3rd) to the E (3rd).

A mean lick using the A blues scale (below). Try to really lay into the E♭ (flattened 5th) for that dirty sound. Notice a sharpened 7th at the end as an embellishment. You can add notes outside of the scale as the mood takes you – try to hear how they're going to sound before you play them.

Track 80
How to play

Scale fingering charts

Common scale patterns you can use for improvisations and melody playing. Play up and down the scales slowly and smoothly until they are memorized. None of the scales here use open strings, so they can be played anywhere on the neck.

▲ A simple, one-octave major scale. Here it's in C, but of course it can be played anywhere.

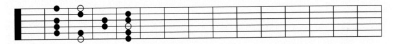

▲ A variation on the previous pattern, this one reaches over two octaves – here it's in G major, although as before can be played anywhere. Keep the fingers on the correct frets.

▲ A two-octave melodic minor scale, starting here on A. This pattern requires some shifting up and down the neck. Compare it with the previous scale pattern and you can clearly see that melodic minor is a major scale with a flattened 3rd.

▲ Now a two-octave harmonic minor scale, a really good finger exercise. This scale creates a very dramatic, 'classical' sound.

▲ Here's a stretch: this version of the A blues reaches over two-and-a-half octaves. You'll need to shift your hand position a couple of times, but this pattern is really worth learning as it's so versatile.

▲ C pentatonic: Finally a variation on the previous shape – this one uses the same notes but begins slightly differently.

Blues progression No 1

The most common chord sequence in rock, blues and jazz, for improvising is the so-called twelve bar blues. The sequence varies depending on the style, but the example below is the basic structure from which other blues sequences stem. You'll notice that every chord is a V^7: In the blues every chord can have a 7th on it – it adds to the crunchy flavour.

Twelve bar blues in G

If you are looking for a single, straightforward scale to play improvised lines over the whole sequence, use the blues scale – in this case the G blues scale (Gm pentatonic with a flattened 5th). The blues scale will see you safely through umpteen choruses of this sequence.

Track 81
Play along

G^7 /	/	/	C^7 /	/	/	G^7 /	/	/	G^7 /	/	/	
C^7 /	/	/	C^7 /	/	/	G^7 /	/	/	G^7 /	/	/	
D^7 /	/	/	C^7 /	/	/	G^7 /	/	/	D^7 /	/	/	‖

If you are looking for a little more detail, and want to use a scale that is specific to the chord over which you are playing, the most common scale choice would be the standard pentatonic scale (with the flattened 3rd added for that 'mean' sound): for this scale you'll want to change whenever the chord changes, so that you are using G pentatonic over G^7, C pentatonic over C^7, and so on. And because these chords all have a flattened 7th in them, that's a note you could easily include in your scale. It's already part of the blues scale, but you'll need to add it to the standard pentatonic scale. The diagram opposite is a variation of the C pentatonic scale on page 143 but now with a flattened 7th, too.

▲ The final D^7 will set you up for another chorus, but if you want to end the music, play another G^7 here to finish.

▲ B B King, the most popular post-war electric blues guitarist famed for his single string and finger vibrato playing.

And the diagram below is for G, slightly altered so it'll fit on the lower frets of the neck: G pentatonic with the flattened 3rd and the flattened 7th:

▲ C pentatonic with the flattened 3rd and flattened 7th.

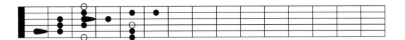

▲ G pentatonic with the flattened 3rd and flattened 7th.

As you become more familiar with the guitar neck and the way these scales are constructed, you'll find your own shapes and patterns. And of course you could combine the scales, switching between G blues and G pentatonic over G^7, for instance. Try the licks from page 142: you could play the A minor lick for C^7, since the A blues and C pentatonic scales are identical.

Blues progression No 2

Here is another blues sequence. This time we are in a minor key, and this is a standard twelve bar minor blues. Let's play it in A minor.

Twelve bar blues in Am

This is a great way to practise those blues scales. Take this slowly, and try to listen out for the difference between the A blues and D blues scales as you play them.

Track 82
Play along

|Am / / / |Am/ / / |Am/ / / |Am/ / / |

|Dm / / / |Dm/ / / |Am/ / / |Am/ / / |

|F⁷ / / / |E⁷/ / / |Am/ / / |E⁷ / / / ‖

And here's an interesting thing. Look at the notes of the F⁷ chord, and notice how the 3rd, 5th and 7th all appear in the A blues scale. Use the A blues scale over the F⁷ chord – but avoid the E of the A blues scale, which would clash horribly with the E♭ in the chord:

◀ The notes of an F⁷ chord – the E♭ appears in the A blues scale as a flattened 5th, but there is no E here, so avoid it or you'll be clashing with the chord.

MUST KNOW

Playing over the dominant

In jazz, blues and rock improvisation, the most discussed chord of all is V⁷, the dominant chord. It's beyond the scope of this book to cover all the options, but if you are interested and want to know more, seek out the so-called 'altered' scale – it includes the root, 3rd and flattened 7th, but also all the alterations: ♭3, #3, ♭5 and #5.

▶ The notes of an E⁷ chord. The G# is an important note and isn't found in the A blues scale – so you might like to try a plain A harmonic minor scale here.

▲ Albert King (1923-1992) was an influential blues guitarist. He taught himself guitar on a home-made instrument.

Now for the E^7: the 3rd of this chord, the G# , is an important note to bring out in your improvisation, so you'll need to use a scale that includes this note. Luckily the note A♭, which is another way of saying G#, is lurking as the flattened 5th of a D blues scale, so you could try that (but you'd need to make sure you stayed away from the A of that scale – it would clash badly with the G#) and other notes of that scale sound very interesting against E^7. You might like to find a scale that contains all the notes of E^7 – so an A harmonic minor would be a good choice here. Here are the notes of the E^7 chord:

want to know **more?**

Take it to the next level...

Go to...
▶ Music notation – pages 112–123
▶ A world of styles – pages 148–173
▶ Guitar essentials – pages 174–185

Other sources
▶ **Your local music shop**
a great starting point for further study: guitar play-along and sheet music and manuals
▶ **Guitar lessons**
whether private lessons or group classes a weekly diary date will focus your study
▶ **Internet**
visit www.allmusic.com or www.cyberfret.com for all your needs

a world

# of styles

A chance to brush up on some authentic guitar styles and on some of the musicians who helped make the different genres famous. From reggae to rock, from folk to jazz, you'll find plenty of tricks and techniques to broaden your repertoire here .

Folk made easy

The acoustic styles of today's folk musicians have a long and rich tradition behind them and Irish and Scottish folk music has been a huge influence on American folk styles such as bluegrass.

Track 83
How to play

Guitar strumming patterns are central to these folk genres, and we'll take a look at some typical sounds. You have already learnt some of the important elements of these styles: Alternating Bass picking, hammer-ons, pull-offs and precise finger-picking are all heavily used.

Alternative tunings are also very common, especially to achieve a 'drone' sound. A drone is essentially a low, continuous note of the kind found on the bagpipes, for example. On the guitar this means that a bass note rings on while other notes change above it.

Here's an example of some drone chords played with the 6th string tuned down to D. The bottom three strings remain open while chords are played over the top. Feel free to play all six strings and let the folky, acoustic quality of the sound ring out. You'll find this kind of shape played by such varied folk guitarists as John Fahey, Dick Gaughan, John Renbourn, John Martyn and James Taylor.

▼ Six drone chords played with the 6th string tuned down to D.

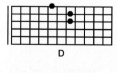

D

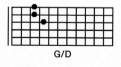

G/D

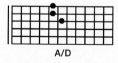

A/D

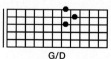

G/D

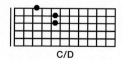

C/D

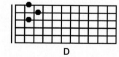

D

◄ John Renbourn founded Pentangle with Bert Jansch and has been an influential figure in English folk music for over three decades.

Previous page: leading exponent of almost all the styles covered in this chapter, guitarist Ry Cooder is known as the archivist of guitar styles.

Embellishing

It's also common to add notes to chords: in the examples below, common chords have been embellished by the inclusion of the 6th, or 9th, for example. Sus chords are also much used. Try stringing these shapes together in various progressions for some strumming practice, and listen to the way the chords become coloured by the additional notes. You could also try hammering on additional notes and pulling them off again later for more colour.

▼ Some common chords embellished.

Cadd9

Gadd2

Dadd2

Aadd2

F#m6/7

G

Asus

Country styles

Track 84
How to play

A good understanding of alternating bass and the kind of passing bass notes encountered on pages 104 and 105 are essential in country guitar.

Country music has such a rich and varied tradition that certain techniques are used in some areas and not in others: it's really impossible to do the music justice in a couple of pages, but here are a couple of recognizable styles from the breadth of country music.

One of the great early country groups, the Carter family, popularized a style known as thumb-lead. Listen, for example, to their famous recordings of Wildwood Flower or Jimmie Brown the Newsboy for Maybelle Carter's classic thumb-lead sound, achieved by playing the melody with the thumb in the bass and punctuating the rhythm with strums in-between.

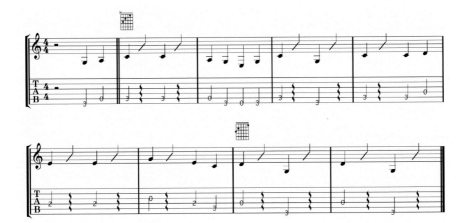

Above is the melody for 'She'll Be Coming Round The Mountain' (see also page 108) in the key of C . It's played entirely by the thumb, and is interspersed with either alternating bass notes or strums. If there is no melody note on the 1st or 3rd beat of the bar, then an alternating bass note is introduced, and if there is no melody note on the 2nd or 4th beat, a strum is played. This way the 'boom-ching, boom-ching' effect of alternating bass is preserved.

As for the top strings, a technique commonly used in country music is to harmonize melody notes in thirds. This sound is reminiscent of Chet Atkins' playing, and is an authentic country-style sound for lead guitar. In the example on page 154, notice how the melody note – the top note in each case – is harmonized by another note below it. The little tune shown overleaf tries to capture the sentimental sound of a country ballad, so play it slowly and imagine a crying pedal steel guitar in the background!

◀ Gillian Welch featured on the soundtrack of Oh Brother, Where Art Thou? as well as having a cameo role in the film.

▲ An adaptation of the first line of 'She'll Be Coming Round The Mountain' (see page 108) in the key of C for thumb-lead style.

MUST KNOW

Inversions
Any interval inverted creates another interval, and the two numbers always add up to nine. A third inverted is a sixth: 3+6=9. A fourth inverted is a fifth: 4+5=9. Try other combinations for yourself. It's a useful rule when you are harmonizing in the manner of the piece overleaf.

A WORLD OF STYLES

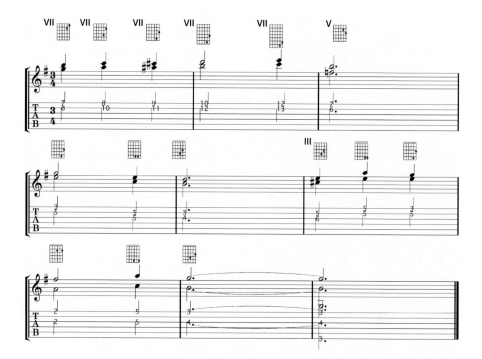

Using very high notes

This piece uses very high notes, right up to the 13th fret! Once you get past the 12th fret, the notes just begin again, so that the note on the 13th fret of the 2nd string will be the same as the 1st fret, a C – and, of course, one octave higher. This piece should be played slowly and smoothly, and when you are confident with the finger positions, you'll find it relatively easy to position the fingers high up the neck where the frets are closer together than at the lower end.

You'll see that in fact the melody isn't strictly always in thirds – in the last three bars, for example, there are sixths. The theory behind this is that, if you were to raise the bottom note of a sixth by an octave, you would have a third. The last pair, G and B, would be a third if the B were an octave higher – or if the G were an octave lower. The sixth, then, is really a third turned

▲ VII, V and III denote the 7th, 5th and 3rd frets respectively.

Track 85
How to play

A WORLD OF STYLES

154

upside down. This is known as an inversion of an interval. If you take a look at the interval used in the 3rd bar, you'll see a tritone has been used, which would suggest a dominant chord. By the way, a tritone inverted is still a tritone.

Chet Atkins often employed this technique of playing melodies in thirds accompanied by a special kind of alternating bass that jumps in octaves rather than fourths and fifths – known as *Travis Picking*, after the great Merle Travis, a pioneer of the style. For some breath-taking examples, check out Merle, Chet, or the younger Australian virtuoso, Tommy Emmanuel.

▲ Emmylou Harris, the queen of country rock, started as a folk singer covering Joni Mitchell songs but was rediscovered by Gram Parsons with whom she recorded. She's gone on, in classic albums and collaborations, to bring a crisp country sensibility to good songs from many other styles and help raised the status of new country.

A WORLD OF STYLES

Rock'n'Roll made easy

With its origins in country and the blues, rock 'n' roll has had a profound effect on popular music. Little Richard, Chuck Berry, Bill Haley and Elvis Presley are among the great names to forge the sound of this all-American phenomenon, and the raw texture of the electric guitar is central to it.

Track 86
How to play

At the heart of rock 'n' roll is the 12-bar blues progression with a heavy, swinging beat. The electric guitar features strongly in reinforcing pounding bass lines or in chunky solo passages full of bent notes and 'double stopping' – playing two strings at once fretted with a single left-hand finger. And for the crisp, attacking sound this is one place you'll really need a plectrum!

Here's an example of a typical rock 'n' roll bass riff, in the guitar-friendly key of E major. This two-bar phrase needs to be played with short, accurate downstrokes.

▼ A characteristic rock 'n' roll bass line – play it crisply and with a little swing (the first note of each pair should last longer than the second)

As the 12-bar blues is such a common structure in rock 'n' roll, you can often play a 2-bar riff like this in a set sequence. Play it twice (for the first 4 bars over chord **I**), and then move the whole phrase up a string for the next 2 bars, over chord **IV**, before returning to the original position for another two bars. Look at a standard blues sequence (pages 144-145) to see how a phrase like this might fit. For the final four bars play just the first part of the phrase in the relevant place, beginning each time on the root of the new chord.

◀ Bo Diddley is a seminal figure in the history of rock 'n'roll, well-known for his custom built guitars and his 'shave-and-a-haircut, six bits' beat which has been mimicked by countless lesser artists. His sound influenced many British players.

With a little practice you'll learn to recognize the sequence and adapt phrases at will. Listen to Chuck Berry's 'Johnny B. Goode' for some great sounding guitar licks, or to Scotty Moore's guitar work on Elvis Presley's early recordings. You'll hear a twanging, gritty guitar sound, playing the sort of lick shown below. The scales used are similar to those used in the blues: pentatonics with ♭3rds and ♭7ths, and of course minor pentatonics with ♭5ths. Whenever pairs of notes are shown, use a single left-hand finger to double-stop the strings. This phrase is in the key of C but of course you could play it elsewhere on the neck for a different key. Try tugging with the left-hand fingers to bend the notes for a more subtle phrasing – and notice how the lick begins with a slide up to the 9th fret of the 3rd string.

Track 87
How to play

▼ A couple of typical licks: don't be afraid to bend the strings to create that bluesy, singing quality. Rock on!

Slide made easy

Slide guitar, or bottleneck guitar, originated in West African instrumental techniques and found its way to America and Europe via the slave trade.

Track 88
Play along

The sound of beer bottles (hence the term 'bottleneck') sliding on guitar strings became a popular sound in the acoustic blues of the American South. Lap steel guitar, a Hawaiian invention, involves resting the guitar on the lap and pressing a metal bar on the strings – and lap steel has found its way into country and bluegrass music.

Lap steel and standard slide players often use alternative 'open' tunings, and slide guitarists generally favour metal cylinders mounted on a left hand finger (either the 3rd or 4th finger) rather than glass bottle necks today. Many people prefer the metal-bodied National Steel guitars for the nutty, biting sound they produce – especially suitable for blues guitarists, and country players favour the Dobro metal-bodied guitars which have more sustain. Either way, slide on a metal bodied guitar produces a wonderful, eerie, plaintive sound that has to be heard to be believed. Listen to Son House, Taj Mahal or Mark Knopfler.

Long before the Buena Vista Social Club became well-known, Ry Cooder helped to popularize the sound of slide guitar in the soundtrack for the film Paris, Texas. For blues slide guitar listen to Robert Johnson's Preachin' Blues or Whiskey Blues, and for great rock slide try Duane Allman – his recording of The Games People Play with saxophonist King Curtis is a classic example of electric slide.

▼ Former guitarist with Jethro Tull and Blodwyn Pig, Mick Abrahams is best known for his power chords. Here he is shown using the slide on his fourth finger.

◄ Michael Messer is a leading British blues influenced slide guitarist. Notice the slide on his third finger.

Open G tuning

Try this open G tuning (starting with the bottom string): D,G,D,G,B,D. This tuning creates a G chord with the open strings (and on the 12th fret, of course). If you slide up to the 5th fret you'll have a C chord, and a D chord on the 7th. Many slide players use this tuning for a blues progression. You could also experiment with the angle of the sliding finger until you can slide on just the top string, or the top two strings while playing the other strings open.

Here's a simple blues progression suitable for this open G tuning with a slide technique:

G (open)	**IG**	**IG**	**IG**	**I**
C (5th fret)	**IC**	**IG** (open)	**IG**	**I**
D (7th fret)	**IC** (5th fret)	**IG** (open)	**IG**	**II**

Funk & reggae made easy

The classic roots reggae guitar sounds of the late 1960s and 1970s derived from the early R & B and Motown styles.

Listen to the Temptations' Ain't Too Proud To Beg for that simple 'm-chank, m-chank' backbeat (2nd and 4th beat) rhythm, played there by Joe Messina, and compare that with the insistent, biting backbeat chops played by Tony Chin on Dennis Brown's Money In My Pocket, a classic reggae track.

Reggae rhythm guitar sounds very dry and sparse. The strumming patterns are generally extremely simple and repetitive: in classic reggae the instruments all have a rôle as percussion instruments. To create that authentic sound try strumming bar chords (higher up the neck to get a sound closer to electric rhythm guitar) and only strum the top three or four strings for a crisp tone. Relaxing the barre as soon as each strum is made stops the notes dead, making that really dry sound. This takes a bit of practise, but it's a technique that is used in all rhythm guitar styles from disco to country to tango. Just release the grip slightly right after the right hand strum to cut off the chord.

Here is a typical reggae strumming pattern, with a variation in the second bar. It looks simple, but timing has to be spot on!

▶ Harare Dread (opposite) is an African reggae master. That really dry sound is made by relaxing the barre as soon as each strum is made stops the notes dead.

Track 89
How to play

A WORLD OF STYLES

Funk guitar shares similar roots, but here the rhythms tend to be much more complex, integrating with the sophisticated bass and drum patterns. Funk music generally uses a beat that subdivides into 16th notes (semiquavers). Here's a typical rhythm, reminiscent of the Tower of Power or Average White Band styles.

▲ Steve Cropper has been hugely influential as a guitarist with Booker T. & the MGs (that's him on Green Onions), with the Blues Brothers in the insane film and subsequent recordings, and with Tower of Power, the tightest funk outfit ever.

And here's what that looks like as a strumming pattern (below). Remember that the rhythm is in 16ths – that's four strums per beat.

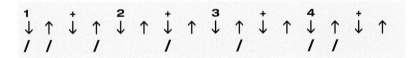

Using a similar touch to the reggae technique, with a dry, chopped sound, but this time subdivided into 16th notes, a funk rhythm guitar part is often delicate and spiky and – don't leave home without one – you'll need a wah-wah pedal to really make it sing.

Track 90
How to play

Hard rock made easy

From the extravagant 60's sound of Jimi Hendrix and Cream, through glam rock and heavy metal, to punk and grunge, the electric guitar has been at the heart of rock. The heavy sound comes largely from the sheer high volume of amplified electric guitars, often accompanied by distortion.

Preferring chunky, in-yer-face major chords, it's often the chord sequence itself that gives rock its character. Although the standard chords **I**, **IV** and **V** are used as elsewhere, a ♭**VII** often plays the role of the dominant chord, with a ♭**III** a bluesy sound. In E these chords might look like this – notice how alternative minor versions are also given for **I**, **IV** and **V**:

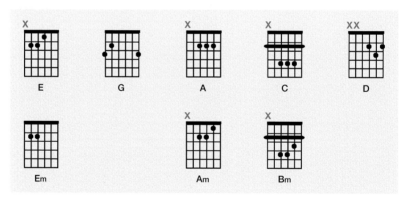

You'll notice that the roots of these chords form an E minor pentatonic scale – E B A B D E, and that you can interchange the major and minor versions of **I**, **IV** and **V** for authentic, gritty sounding heavy rock sequences. Try the sequences below, then feel free to experiment: chop and change chords to hear the way they react with each other. The root movement – the bass line from the root of one chord to the root

▲ Standard heavy rock chords in the key of E.

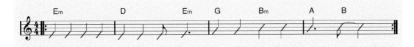

▲ A simple rock sequence in the key of E – notice the chords of D and G, which aren't in they key of E, but the roots of these chords are within E minor pentatonic.

▲ This sequence begins on Em. The chord of D, the ♭VII, gives the sequence an almost medieval quality.

▲ Here's one that's nominally in A, but the chords used are from the D minor pentatonic scale, hence the F. The last two bars, with chords stepping up in tones (F-G-A) gives the sequence a very grandiose feel.

of the next, is the real 'melody' here. If you have an electric guitar and amplifier, crank it up and practise those Pete Townsend windmill strums!

Power chords

Many rock guitarists favour chords that have no 3rd, which means that they are neither major nor minor, having only the root and 5th. These ambiguous chords are often played on just two or three strings, and – because of the drive and energy these shapes convey – are known as power chords. They are generally written with a '5' after the root name: E5, A5, etc.

▲ Gary Moore, the ex Thin Lizzy guitarist epitomizes hard rock and heavy metal guitar with a heavy blues twist. Check out his blistering solo on the single 'Parisienne Walkways' and his guitar work on his own album 'After Hours'.

Here are some typical 3-string and 2-string power chord shapes starting on the 6th, 5th or 4th strings, including some that are actually just pairs of notes an octave apart:

▼ As there are no open strings used, all these shapes can of course be moved up and down the neck to change the pitch.

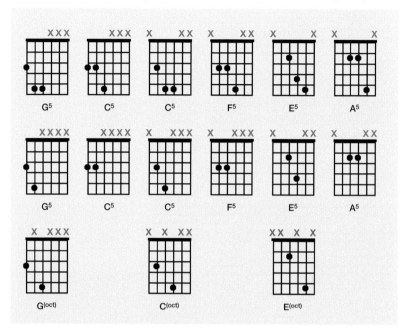

Now here's an exercise using a single power chord shape. Mute the unwanted strings by gently resting the side of the right-hand little finger on the upper strings near the bridge. Every strum should be a down stroke, preferably with a plectrum, to get that really abrasive rock sound. Rock on!

Track 91
Play along

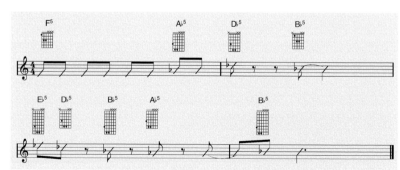

Latin Rhythms

Music from South America and the Caribbean, especially Brazil and Cuba, has become extremely popular, influencing pop and jazz for the last 50 years.

We'll look at two styles, representative of the sort of rhythms you are likely to encounter in the Latin vein: the bossa nova from Brazil, and the rumba from Cuba.

Bossa nova

Bossa nova originated in Brazil in the late 1950s and by the early 1960s the bossa nova craze had swept Europe and the U.S. Recordings by Joao Gilberto and Stan Getz with Astrid Gilberto of songs such as 'Girl from Ipanema' and 'Desafinado' were huge hits, and the sound is still extremely popular. Several rhythmic elements define bossa nova, including a persistent soft shaker, but the most distinctive percussion is played on the cláve, (pronounced kla-veh), a pair of hand-held wooden sticks struck together. Below is the basic rhythm of the cláve – if ever you are playing bossa nova in a group, make sure someone is beating this out on the back of a guitar, a bottle, on the table...

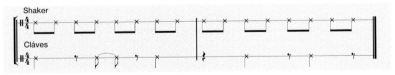

The music uses lots of jazz-type chords – see page 170 – with meandering, gentle melodies.

A typical picking pattern for the guitar is shown overleaf: this sounds especially good on a nylon-strung, classical-style guitar. Alternating bass works really well here, too.

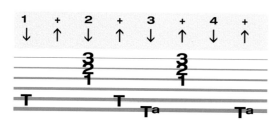

◀ A typical bossa nova picking, with optional alternating bass. This is written out for a 5-string chord, such as C^7.

Track 92
How to play

Experiment by picking the 2nd, 3rd and 4th strings, rather than the top three, for a mellower sound. You'll come across chords in bossa nova that use flattened or raised 5ths – these chords aren't suitable for alternating bass, but standard major and minor chords will sound great played this way.

Here's another pattern you could try. This time we'll use the hand slap we looked at on page 94. But rather than a full-on percussive noise with the hand, try bringing just the finger-tips down onto the strings – bring each finger down onto the string on which it belongs for the pattern, so you're ready to pick again as soon as you need to. This one is a little trickier, you might have to spend a while going round and round on it until it's smooth and relaxed – but the extra effort is really worth it.

◀ Another bossa nova rhythm, again with alternating bass: tap gently with the finger-tips on beats 2 and 4.

Track 93
How to play

Rumba

The rumba originated in Cuba from a combination of African and Spanish influences. There are various styles of rumba from the sedate yambu and the passionate guaguanco to the sometimes wild columbia, with its acrobatic and daring moves.

Rumba strumming patterns

The versions shown below are suitable for accompanying vocalists or instrumentalists and if you get this off pat, you should have a lot of fun with it. The strumming patterns below are as follows: the first one has hand slaps on the 2nd and 4th beats – try to make these as distinct and regular as possible. You'll notice we've added a little arrow at the beginning of the first strum: begin the down stroke slightly early and take a little longer moving your right hand across the strings, as though you are raking the hand across. This will, of course, mean that you have to recover quickly from the upstroke on the last half-beat of the bar. The idea is to hear each string individually as though you were strumming a harp – dig into the strings as you go across them for a really meaty, dramatic sound.

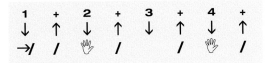

◀ A rumba rhythm that relies on a heavily anticipated first beat.

Track 94
How to play

The anticipated first beat is in fact the only down stroke played in the pattern: the 2nd and 4th beats have slaps, and the 3rd beat is silent. Let the upstroke before the 3rd beat ring out – emphasise it and keep the hand away until the next upstroke.

The example below has the hand slap on the second beat only.

Track 95
How to play

◀ Another rumba rhythm: aim for a dry, clipped sound for that authentic Cuban beat. The rumba popular in Europe and the USA is really a watered down version of the traditional dance – the original has fantastically complex percussion rhythms on the congas and on the cajon, a large packing case played as a deep drum.

This time we have an anticipated down stroke on the 2nd beat, and the slap has moved to the 3rd beat. Try playing the other strums as rigidly as possible to get a really tight, clipped rhythm.

Alternative tunings

Although guitar students all begin with the standard E-A-D-G-B-E tuning, advanced guitarists often change the tuning of one or more of the strings to achieve a specific effect.

Tracks 96&97
How to play

Drop D: D A D G B E

We looked at this tuning in the folk section (page 150): it's known as 'drop D' tuning. It's great for playing in the key of D, and it's easy to adapt chords from regular tuning. Here is a sample of the important drop D chords:

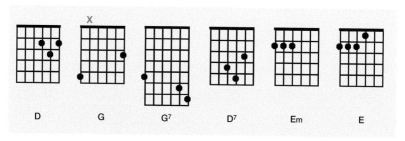

D   G   G⁷   D⁷   Em   E

Drop D, drop G: D G D G B E

Once you're familiar with the idea of a 6th string tuned to D, it's time to take it a little further. For playing in the key of G, especially in a folk and blues style, you can also drop the 5th string to G. This tuning gives you a droning D in the bass for any G chords, or you can omit the 6th string. Some useful shapes:

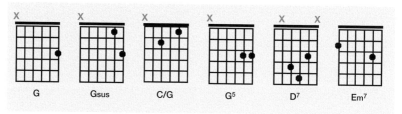

G   Gsus   C/G   G⁵   D⁷   Em⁷

Open G: D G D G B D

It's now just a small step to an open tuning we looked at in the section on slide guitar – all the open strings together make a simple chord of G. This tuning is a favourite of finger-pickers everywhere, and if you want to hear open G in action, listen to the Rolling Stones' Wild Horses. There are plenty of straightforward chords you can play in this tuning, and a number of other colourful chords with notes added. Play a barre on any fret for a major chord, and add a finger three frets higher on the 4th string for a dominant seventh chord. Here's a small number of the many chords that bring out the flavour of this tuning:

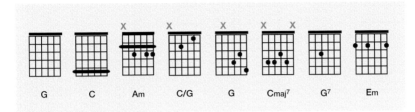

G   C   Am   C/G   G   Cmaj⁷   G⁷   Em

Open D: D A D F# A D

An alternative open tuning is open D, in which the open strings make a simple D chord. Another great favourite of slide players but equally suitable for picking or strumming on acoustic or electric guitar. The unusual tonal character of many of the chords comes from the 'forgiving' approach: guitarists using alternative tunings often include additional notes in the chord that make the shape easier to play, so you'll often play chords with 9ths, 11ths and 13ths in them. Some favourite open D chords are below:

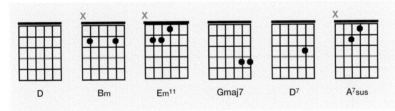

D   Bm   Em¹¹   Gmaj7   D⁷   A⁷sus

'DADGAD'

As the name suggests, this tuning uses the notes D A D G A D. It's extremely popular with guitarists playing Irish styles, and is a kind of hybrid tuning using elements of open D and open G. Study the open D tuning until you are comfortable and you'll be well placed to appreciate the versatile sonorous character of 'DADGAD'. Here are a few classic 'DADGAD' shapes:

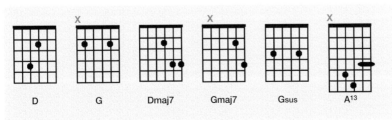

D   G   Dmaj7   Gmaj7   Gsus   A¹³

Jazz made easy

For many people, jazz is the most sophisticated of all styles, bringing together a understanding of theoretical, technical and aesthetic skills.

Precise picking

Many jazz guitarists prefer to play an *archtop semi-acoustic* guitar such as the Gibson L-5, and almost all use a small, firm plectrum for precise picking of the strings. Great jazz guitarists to listen to include Charlie Christian (the father of amplified jazz guitar), Joe Pass, Wes Montgomery, Jim Hall, Barney Kessel, and Django Reinhardt.

As well as a good understanding of scales, it is essential for the jazz guitarist to have a comprehensive collection of chord shapes with various *altered extensions*, and a firm rhythmic sense. Jazz guitarists often accompany singers and need to be able to provide solid melodic and rhythmic support to a vocalist. On page 173 a song that you've already played has been re-arranged with some jazz-style chords and substitutions. Many jazz chord shapes only use four strings: they can be played by the four fingers of the left hand and the strings can be picked individually, making them versatile as they can be played anywhere on the neck.

▲ Barney Kessel (1923–2004) with a Gibson L-5. Top LA session guitarists Larry Carlton and Lee Ritenour share a great affinity with this jazz guitarist.

▼ All the notes of a C major scale arranged in order of thirds. Notice that every note after the root is referred to as an odd number.

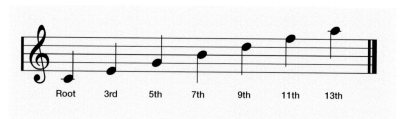

Root   3rd   5th   7th   9th   11th   13th

Extensions

Extensions are extra notes added to a chord to make it more colourful: we looked at building chords previously, where we got as far as making four-note chords, up to the 7th (see page 132). However, it is possible to keep going up in thirds until all the notes of the scale have been included (see opposite below).

Often a jazz musician will 'alter' (sharpen or flatten) the extensions to further colour a chord. Here are altered extensions available to add to a C chord:

▼ The root and 3rd with possible additions and replacements for chord notes in C. Certain notes have more than one name: compare for instance the flattened 5th with the sharpened 11th, or the sharpened 5th with the flattened 13th.

Root   3rd   flat 5th   sharp 5th   flat 7th   flat 9th   sharp 9th   sharp 11th   flat 13th

The different names for the same notes can get a bit confusing, and a full explanation of jazz chords is outside the scope of this book. But a sharpened 5th or flattened 13th makes an augmented chord, sometimes signified by a + sign. So $C^7\#5$, C^7+, $C^7\flat13$ and C^7aug are essentially identical: the notes in C would be C, E, G# and B♭.

Diminished chord

A chord not mentioned so far is the diminished chord, which has a flattened 3rd, a flattened 5th and a double flattened 7th (!) The notes in C would be C, E♭, G♭ and A. It's a useful shape and you'll find it overleaf. As the diminished chord contains notes that are all a minor 3rd apart from each other, you can start on any note and achieve the same chord, so C diminished is the same as E♭ diminished, or G♭ diminished, or A diminished. The diminished chord is written 'dim' (e.g. C dim) or with a small circle after the chord name like this: C° (see page 173).

MUST KNOW

6th or 13th?
The 13th is in fact the 6th note of the scale. Where it is included without a 7th in the chord it is known as the 6th. Likewise the 9th, which is the 2nd note of the scale, is called the 2nd only if the chord contains no 7th. The 11th is the 4th of the scale and the same rules apply.

A WORLD OF STYLES

171

Danny Boy – jazz style

A number of jazz-style chords are written out
below. Try playing them smoothly and gently.
The stretches might seem a bit tricky at first but
they are all perfectly playable with a little practice.
They are among the most commonly used jazz
chord shapes – but there are many more!

Track 98
How to play

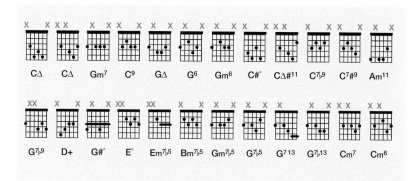

Bear in mind that all of these chords can be
played anywhere on the neck depending on the
required pitch.

▼ Tal Farlow (1921-1998),
one of the greats of the
modern jazz guitar. He also
wrote his own guitar
instruction book.

C△ / / /	Gm⁷ / C⁹ /	F△ / / /	Fm⁶ / / /
Oh, Danny Boy,	the pipes, the pipes are	call - ing.	From glen to

C△ / E⁷#⁹/	Am⁷ / Am⁶/	D⁹ / / /	G⁷♭5/ / /
Glen, and -	down the mountain	- side.	The su - mmer's

C△ / / /	Gm⁷/ F#⁷♭5/	F△ / / /	F#°/ / /
Gone and	all the rose - s	dy - ing.	Tis you, tis

C△ / A⁷♭13 /	Dm⁷/ G⁷ 13/	C△ / A♭△ /	C△ / G⁷ 13/
You, must	go and I must	bide.	But come ye

F#⁷♭5 / / /	F△ / / /	C△ / Dm⁷Em⁷	Bm⁷♭5 / E⁷♭9/
Back when	summer's in the	mea - dow,	or when the

Am⁷ / Am⁶/	F△ / A⁷ 13/	D⁷ / / /	G⁷ 13/ G⁷♭13/
Va lley's	hushed and white with	snow.	Tis I'll be

C△ / Em⁷♭5/	F△ / F#° /	C△ / / /	Fm⁷/ / /
Here in	sun- shine or in	sha - dow,	oh Dann -y

C△ / C#° /	Dm⁷/ G⁷ 13/	A♭△/ D♭△ /	C△#11/ / /
Boy oh Dann - y	Boy I love you	so.	

Try using some of the above shapes in this song – feel free to experiment and *alter* and *substitute* chords as you see fit.

Though in jazz a regular picking pattern is less common, to provide a suitable rhythmic framework for these chords you might try something simple along the lines of the pattern below, taken from our version of All Through the Night.

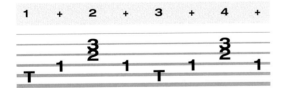

Finally, a note on new symbols: the circle ° is more commonly used than 'dim' for a diminished chord in jazz, and the triangle △ is often used to denote a maj7 chord: these are the symbols you'll see till the end of the book.

want to know **more?**

Take it to the next level...

Go to...
- ▶ **Guitar essentials** – pages 176–185
- ▶ **Further techniques** – pages 92–109
- ▶ **Music notation** – pages 112–123

Other sources
- ▶ **Your local music shop**
  a great starting point for further study of guitar music styles
- ▶ **Live gigs**
  go to as many as you can to get a feel for how the great guitarists do it
- ▶ **Internet**
  visit www.allmusic.com or www.guitarsite.com or www.wholenote.com for all your needs

guitar

essentials

We'll close up by taking a look at guitar maintenance and some other resources such as publications and websites to take your study to the next level. Finally, in case you still can't tell a crotchet from a hatchet, there's a glossary to help you out, plus a useful at-a-glance recap of the major chord diagrams for handy reference.

Changing strings

Sooner or later the strings on your guitar will become worn and jaded, and the sound they produce will no longer be bright and crisp. Alternatively, a string might snap through natural wear and tear or over-zealous strumming. Either way it's time for new strings, and we'll have a look at the process of removing an old string from a steel-strung guitar, and replacing it with a new one.

Change them all in one session

Ideally, all the strings should be changed together. This way, all the strings will be nice and bright together, and having the guitar temporarily string-free means you can do a little cleaning of the fingerboard – and you can easily retrieve any plectrums that may have fallen into the sound hole!

The first thing to do is to loosen all the strings by detuning them until they are floppy. A string winder – a small plastic crank designed for this job – will be a big help and save the wrist-ache that can result from lots of winding. (You can see it clearly in the picture opposite, top right.)

Once all the strings are nice and loose, pull off the bottom pin (6th string) from the saddle ❶. The string winder has a little notch to help with this job, but you could use a thin flat object such as a wooden ruler. Don't be tempted to use scissors, a knife, or pliers as they will mark the pin and saddle and may even damage the guitar. Coil up the old string and dispose of it safely – the end might be sharp, so be sure to wind it in. Some people keep old strings for spares, but it's better to keep a new packet for spares.

Remove the new string from the packet and insert the ball end into the saddle hole, replacing the pin ❷. Be sure that the string sits in the groove along the shaft of the pin.

WATCH OUT

Classical restringing

Restringing on a classical guitar is similar, except the strings attach to the saddle via a knot that's easy to do but difficult to describe. Ask your local music shop to show you how and check the string is wound in the correct direction around the drum of the tuning peg.

Once the pin is securely in place (press it gently home with the thumb) thread the other end of the string through the hole in the machine head ❸ and pull it through until there is enough slack for the string to be wound around the machine head pin two or three times.

Now you can start winding the string up, holding the string gently in the groove of the nut ❹. Make sure that the slack is taken up with the pin turning anti-clockwise for the bottom three strings, and clockwise for the top three strings. If you're in doubt, look at the way the other strings are wound before you remove them.

Hopefully, after two or three complete turns of the machine head pin the string will be taught. Don't worry about tuning for now, as you should have all the strings in place before you tune up. When all the strings are installed, trim the floppy ends with a snip (take care not to cut the tight string by mistake), cutting them close to the pin ❺. The top ends can be sharp so be careful here.

Finally, when all the new strings are in place, correctly wound and trimmed, it's time to tune them up. New strings have a lot of excess elasticity in them when they are first put on the guitar, so you'll have to keep retuning the guitar over a period of a few days, but eventually they'll settle down and you'll be ready to enjoy the gorgeous sound of a set of new strings. For how to tune, refer back to pages 22-23.

Simple maintenance

There is a bewildering array of products on the market claimed to be 'good' for your guitar. Some of them are genuinely useful but the most important things you'll need to take care of your guitar are a little time and elbow grease.

Dirt and grime

Dirt and grime are the enemy of bright-sounding strings, and you should always wash your hands thoroughly before playing – and never eat or drink while you play. Keeping your strings clean will help them to sound fresh, and there's nothing nastier than playing strings that are sticky and grubby.

Perspiration from your hands will inevitably find its way onto your strings, and a simple wipe with a lint-free cloth after playing should take care of it: keep a cloth in your guitar case.

Many products exist to make your strings 'faster' – these are essentially de-greasers, often lemon-based, that cut through the grime that can build up on the strings.

◀ Just a few of the many products available to keep your guitar healthy.

Never use furniture polish on your guitar! The wax residue it leaves will not improve the sound and will clog up the strings. Special guitar polish is available, but a simple wipe with a clean cloth is probably all you will need.

Looking after your guitar

Finally, a few basic rules you should follow to keep your guitar in good shape: try to avoid direct sunlight, and try to avoid radiators: if you keep your guitar in a centrally-heated room, take steps to ensure that the air is not too dry. Also try to avoid rapid changes of humidity and temperature: if you are moving your guitar from one extreme to another, leave it in its case for a while before bringing it out. You should never lean your guitar against a chair or wall – more guitars come to grief this way than any other, and it's easy enough to put the guitar on a stand or in its case when it's not in use. If you are storing your guitar for a while or putting it in transit, be sure to loosen the strings to take the strain off the neck.

▲ A guitar stand is a very useful accessory for preventing accidental knocks and kicks.

▼ A simple wipe with a cloth will keep your guitar grime-free.

Chords at a glance

On these pages you'll find some of the most common – and some not-so common – chord shapes, arranged in rough alphabetical order for ready reference. You will have come across many of them in this book but some others are included to whet your appetite for further study. Good luck!

▼▶ + = aug (augmented), Δ = maj^7 (major 7th), ^{O} = dim (diminished), $^\emptyset$ = m$^{7\flat5}$ (half diminished)

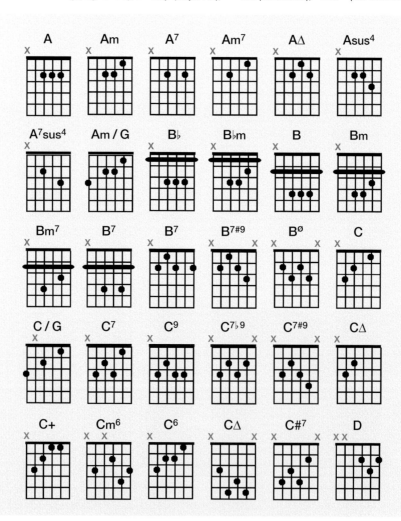

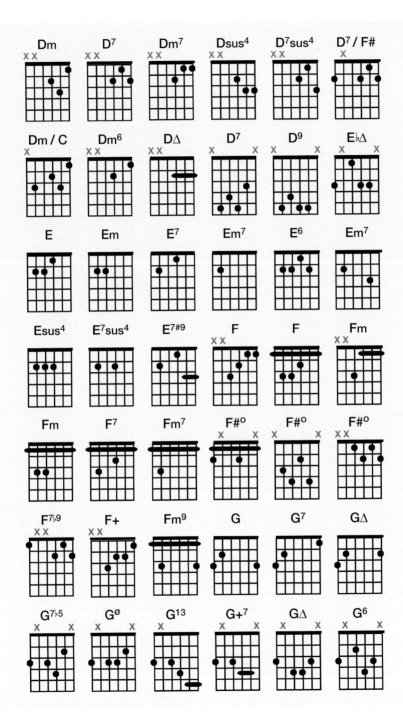

Glossary of terms

Accidental
A temporary sharp or flat

Altered
A sharpened or flattened chord extension
e.g. $\#^9$, $\flat^{13}$

Alternating bass
Bass line that switches from the tonic to the dominant of the chord

Anticipation
Playing slightly ahead of the beat

Archtop
A curve-bellied style of acoustic and semi-acoustic guitar, typically for jazz

Arpeggio
Notes of a chord played in sequence

Articulation
Manner in which a note is played: detached, smooth, with attack, etc.

Augmented
Raised by a semitone (e.g. augmented 5th); chord with a sharpened 5th, often written with a + (e.g. C7+)

Backbeat
2nd and 4th beats of the bar in popular music

Bar (beats in the)
Group of regular pulses, as in 'four in the bar'. Also called 'measure' (USA)

Bar (chord)
Chord in which the first finger forms a barre (see below)

Barre
A grip, usually by the first finger, across several strings on the same fret

Bass
Low pitch notes; also the bottom notes of a chord sequence, as in 'bass line'

Beat
Rhythmic pulse

Blues Scale
Minor pentatonic scale with a flattened 5th

Bottom
Lowest-pitched note; 6th string

Capo - short for Capodastre, a small elasticated or sprung grip fitting over the fingerboard for a barre

Chord
Notes played simultaneously

Chromatic
Using all notes; a sequence of semitones

Cláves
Pair of wooden sticks used in Latin American percussion

Common time
4 beats to the bar; 4/4

Crescendo
Gradual increase of volume

Crotchet
Note representing one beat in 4/4 time

Diatonic
Of the key

Diminished
Lowered by a semitone; also a chord comprising four minor 3rds

Diminuendo
Gradual decrease of volume

Dissonance
Clashing notes e.g. two notes a semitone or a tritone apart

Dominant – see Fifth

Dominant-tonic relationship
Phenomenon of chord $\mathbf{V}^7$ resolving to chord $\mathbf{I}$

Double stopping
Playing across two strings with one left-hand finger

Downbeat
First beat of the bar

Drone
Continuous bass note playing below changing chords

Dynamic markings
Symbols in musical notation denoting volume and changes in volume

Dynamics
Volume and changes in volume

Eighth note
American term for quaver

Extensions
Upper notes added to a chord above the 7th e.g. 9th, 11th, 13th

Fifth
Fifth note of the scale, also known as the dominant; interval between the first and fifth notes of a major scale (7 semitones); upper note of a triad; 5th chord of a key

Flat
Too low (tuning); a semitone lower (e.g. B♭); the symbol '♭'

Forte
Loud (Italian = strong)

Golpe
Flamenco technique of tapping the front of the guitar with the right hand whilst strumming

Half Note
American term for minim

Headstock
End of the guitar neck holding the tuning mechanisms

Interval
Distance (of pitch) between two notes

Inversion
An upturned interval, in which one note is moved by an octave

Key
Tonality; pertaining to a specific scale

Key signature
Number of sharps or flats in a key

Ledger line
Additional lines above or below the staff to accommodate high or low notes

Lick(s)
Prepared phrases for improvisation

Machine head
Tuning mechanism for a steel-string guitar

Major
Pertaining to the major scale

Mezzo
Moderately (Italian = half)

Minim
Note representing two beats in 4/4

Minor
Pertaining to the minor scale

Natural
Not sharp or flat

Octave
Interval of twelve semitones

Open (string)
Without fretting

Open tuning
Tuning in which a simple chord can be played without fretting any notes

Passing notes
Often in bass lines, notes stepping between two others

Pentatonic
(Scale) having five notes

Piano
Soft (Italian = soft)

Pick-up
Electronic device to amplify sound, usually under the strings or beneath the bridge

Pitch
Height of a note

Quarter note
American term for crotchet

Quaver
Note representing a half of a beat in 4/4

Rag
Jazzy style piece using syncopation

Relative minor
Minor key or minor scale sharing its key signature with a major key or major scale

Repeat
Section played twice or more

Resolve (dominant-tonic relationship)
End tension (caused by the dissonance of the dominant chord) by playing the tonic chord

Riff
Repeated rhythmic phrase in jazz, blues and rock

Root
Bottom note of a scale or chord

Scalar
Step-wise, up or down a scale

Scale
Sequence of notes, arranged in ascending or descending pitch

Secondary dominant
Dominant (V^7) of the true V^7 of a key

Semi-acoustic
Acoustic guitar with a pick-up

Semibreve
Note representing a whole bar in 4/4
Semiquaver
Note representing a quarter of a beat in 4/4
Semitone
Twelfth of an octave; the distance in pitch from one fret to the next on the guitar
Sharp
Too high (tuning); a semitone higher (e.g. C#); the symbol '#'
Sixteenth note
American term for semiquaver
Slash chord
Chord in which the bass note is not the root
Staff
Five-lined grid for music notation
Staves
Plural of staff
Structure
Form
Substitution
Replacement chord, occurring often in jazz
Syncopation
Emphasizing off-beats, much used in jazz

Tempo
Speed

Tension
In chords, feeling created by dissonance
Time signature
Number and type of beat used as the basis for the rhythmic framework of a piece
Thumb-lead
Melodic bass picking style
Tone
Timbre; interval of 2 semitones
Tonic – see Root
Top
High-pitched note; first string
Transpose
Arrange in a new key
Travis picking
Picking style popularised by Merle Travis
Triplet
Group of three notes subdividing a beat
Tritone
Half an octave; interval of 6 semitones

Upbeat
Last beat of the bar; the beat before the beginning of a piece of music

Whole note
American term for semibreve

Need to know more?

Bibliography

Acoustic Guitar Magazine (Ed), *Flatpicking Guitar Essentials* (String Letter Publishing)
A great collection of play-along exercises in various styles – each chapter is written by a different specialist in the genre.

Baker, Mickey *Mickey Baker's Jazz Guitar* (Omnibus Press 1999)
The best-selling jazz guitar method, full of great ideas.

Bennett, Joe *Guitar on Tap* (Omnibus 2001)
A pocketbook stuffed full of useful tips and tricks.

Grossman, Stefan *Fingerpicking Guitar Solos* (Chappell 1979)
A collection of fingerpicking arrangements by legends of the style including Duck Baker and John James.

McQuaid, Sarah *The Irish DADGAD Guitar Book* (Ossian 1995}
An excellent introduction to the wonderful world of DADGAD tuning as used in Irish music.

Silverman, Jerry *The Folksinger's Guitar Guide (Volumes 1 & 2)* (Oak 1964)
Still going strong, these books date from the folk revival of the 1960s and cover North American folk styles with clarity and some great music.

Star, Orrin *Hot Licks for Bluegrass Guitar* (Oak 1985)
If you're serious about bluegrass lead guitar, this is the book for you.

Stetina, Troy *Total Rock Guitar* (Hal Leonard Publishing Corp 2001)
Does what it says on the cover!

Traum, Happy *Bluegrass Guitar* (Oak 1974)
Fingerpicking and lead styles comprehensively covered.

A selection of useful websites:

www.stetina.com/
The official website of Troy Stetina, one of the most popular educators in heavy rock.

www.theguitarfiles.com/
A good, general guitar resource.

www.wholenote.com/
Huge online resource with lessons, licks, downloads and more.

www.bangingsticks.com/
Apart from anything else, the easiest place on the web to tune your guitar.

www.members.aol.com/sokolowmus/
A full listing of Fred Sokolow's respected series of guitar tuition books.

www.guitarscalesmethod.com/
Want to learn your scales effectively?

www.traditionalmusic.co.uk/
An archive of traditional and folk music from mainly Britain and Ireland.

www.actiontab.com/
The home of interactive play-along graphics: hard to imagine but a joy to use.

www.thetabworld.com/
Searchable tablature library and much more.

www.dolmetsch.com/
Extremely useful resource including a truly excellent guide to music theory.

www.harmony-central.com/
One of the best-known music resource sites, with links to OLGA, the Online Guitar Archive, for a huge selection of guitar tablature.

www.sosyourmom.com/
A lively band site with a fine resource of Irish traditional music in notation and MIDI formats.

www.torvund.net/guitar/
An online guitar resource with a good selection of clear tutorials.

www.guitargallerymusic.com/
A good one-stop shop for guitar music.

Index

Song titles are in *italics*

Abrahams, Mick 158
accessories 20-1
accidental, an 119
acoustic guitar
    parts of 7
    types 16
'action', the 17
aeolian mode 137
All through the night 64-5
Allman, Duane 158
'altered' scale 146
alternating bass 64-5, 66-7, 68-9, 70-1,
        76, 104, 106-7, 152
alternative tunings 168-9
Amazing grace 50-1
archtop guitar 170
Ar Hyd V Nos 64
articulation 112
Atkins, Chet 153, 155
Autrey, Gene 82
Average White Band 161

Baez, Joan 78, 89
Banks of the Ohio 70-1
bar chords 74-91, 130
    A⁷ 86, 87
    Bm 84
    B⁷ 81, 84
    C 75, 76, 78, 86, 87
    C⁷ 82
    D⁷ 77, 86
    F 74, 76, 78, 80
    G 80, 86
    G⁷ 76, 78
    achieving well-balanced 75
    difference between using a
            capo and 88
    practising 82
bass note *see* alternating bass
Berlioz, Hector 120
Berry, Chuck 156, 157
Blind Boys of Alabama 38
Bluegrass picking 104-5
blues improvisation 140-7
    twelve bar blues in Am 146-7
    twelve bar blues in G 144-5

blues scale 139, 140, 141,142, 144
bossa nova 165-6
bottleneck guitar 158-9
bridging 57
Brightman, Sarah 90
Butler, Bernard 10
buying a guitar 16-17

capos (capodastres) 21, 75, 88-9, 90-1
Careless love 68-9
Carlton, Larry 170
Carter family 152
cases, guitar 20
Cash, Johnny 32, 68, 78, 86
Cassidy, Eva 58
Chieftains 34
choosing a guitar 16-17
chords 11, 31, 129, 131
    at a glance 178-9
    A 50, 66, 71, 75
    Am 40, 41, 48, 66
    A⁷ 32, 33
    Am⁷ 31, 59
    B⁷ 40, 67
    C 12, 34, 35, 36, 41, 66, 68, 79
    C⁷ 58
    D 32, 33, 46, 71
    Dm 34
    D⁷ 31, 41, 62-3, 66, 77
    Dsus 61
    E 48, 67, 68, 71, 74, 76
    Em 40, 60
    E⁷ 46, 47
    F 56, 57, 68, 69
    G 32, 33, 38-9, 40, 41, 64, 67, 68
    G⁷ 36-7, 41, 79
    V⁷ 132-3, 146
    changing from one to another 34, 49
    cleaning 178-9
    common time 115
    diminished 171
    embellishing of 151
    extensions to 171
    three-note (triads) 129-31
    four-note 132-3, 171
    4-string 31, 33
    5-string 31, 33
    power 163-4

chords (cont.)
    sus 61, 85, 151
    see also bar chords
chromatic passing notes 105
Circle of Fifths 128, 133
Clapton, Eric 29, 32
classical (or Spanish) guitar 16-17
cláve 165
clef 113
Cockles and mussels 62-3
common time 115
composition 134-5
Cooder, Ry 151, 158
country styles 152-5
crescendo 120
Cream 162
Cropper, Steve 161
crotchet (quarter note) 113
customized picking 106-7

DADGAD 169
Daisy, Daisy 76-7
Danny boy 58-9,
    jazz style 172-3
Davis, Rev. Gary 123
Denver, John 82
diatonic chords 131
Diddley, Bo 157
diminished chords 171
diminuendo 120
dominant chord (V7) 146
dominant-tonic relationship 36, 79, 83,
    132-3
dorian mode 137
dotted notes 114
double stopping 156
'down' 30
Down by the riverside 38-9
down stroke 44
Dread, Harare 160
drone 150
drop D tuning 150, 168
drop D, drop G tuning 168
Drunken sailor 34-5
Dylan, Bob 16, 68, 70
dynamics 112, 120

Early One Morning 90-1
eighth note *see* quavers
electric guitar 17
    parts of 8
extensions 171

Farlow, Tal 172
Fender-style guitars 8
finger and thumb positions 12, 28-9, 54
fist strokes 94-5
Flatt, Lester 106
flats 115, 118, 128
folk music 10-11, 150-1
'forte' 120
four-note chords 132-3, 171
Franklin, Aretha 50
funk 161

Gingernut Rag 122-3
glam rock 162
glossary 180-2
Golpe 94
Greensleeves 84-5
Grossman, Stefan 123
Grunge 162
Guthrie, Arlo 78

Haley, Bill 156
half note (minim) 113
hammer-ons 100, 102-3
hand positions 28-9
hand slap 94-5, 166
hard rock 162-4
Harris, Emmylou 155
headstock 8
Hendrix, Jimi 162
Henry VIII, 84
He's got the whole world 36-7
Home on the range 82-3
Hurt, Mississippi John 123

interval 126
inversions of an interval 153, 154
Irish washerwoman, The 98-9

Jansch, Bert 10, 151
jazz 170-3
John Brown's body 40-1
Johnson, Robert 158
Joplin, Janis 68
Jones, George 106

Kessel, Barney 170
key signatures 118, 128
King, Albert 147

Latin rhythms 165-7
lead guitar 140
ledger lines 112
left-hand finger numbers 12, 29
licks 141, 142, 157
Lynn, Loretta 36

maintenance, guitar 168-9
major scales 126-8, 138
Malone, Molly 62
Mama don't allow 96-7
Manhattan Transfer 122
Marr, Johnny 10
Messer, Michael 159
metal, heavy 162
metronomes 21
mezzo 120
mezzopiano 120
minim (half note) 113
minor scales 128, 136-7
mirror image 33
Mississippi John Hurt 123
modes 137
    aeolian 137
    dorian 137
Moore, Gary 29, 163
Moore, Scotty 157
music shops 9
muting 95
My grandfather's clock 86-7

Nelson, Willie 16, 29
Newton John, Olivia 70
notation 104, 112-23, 128
    displaying note values 113
    dotted notes 114
    repeats 116
    sharps and flats 115, 128
    and staff 112
    tablature 117, 118-19
    tails up and tails down 119
    and time signatures 114, 115

O sole mio 48-9
off beat 46
Oh Susannah 56-7
open D tuning 169
open G tuning 159, 168
Owens, Buck 106

palm strokes 95
passing notes 104, 105

patterns, naming 65
pause symbol 120
Pentangle 151
pentatonic scale 138-9, 141, 142, 144-5
Peter, Paul and Mary 64
'piano' 120
pick-ups 37
picking 54-71
    alternating bass note 64-5, 68-9
    basic technique 55
    Bluegrass 104-5
    customized 106-7
    on every half-beat 58-9
    hammer-on and pull-offs 100-1
    modifying patterns 62-3
    patterns 13
    precise 170
    Travis 155
    two-string 60-1
picks 20
posture 26-7
practising 6, 8, 11
precise picking 170
Presley, Elvis 32, 48, 50, 68,156
pull-offs 101, 103
punk 162

quarter note (crotchet) 113
quavers (eighth note) 113, 123

reggae 160-1
Renbourn, John 151
repeats 116
restringing 19, 176-7
right-hand finger numbers 28, 54
Richard, Little 156
Ritenour, Lee 170
rock, hard 162-3
rock 'n' roll style 156-7
Rogers, Roy 82
Rollin' in my sweet baby's arms 106-8
Rowan, Peter 97
rumba 166-7

scalar passing notes 105
scales 126-8
    blues 139, 140, 141, 142,144
    E minor 136-7
    F major 127
    G major 127, 137
    fingering charts 143
    and licks 141, 142

scales (cont.)
    major 126-8, 138
    minor 128, 136-7
    modes 137
    pentatonic 138-9, 141, 142, 144-5
Scarborough Fair 60-1
Scruggs, Earl 106
Seeger, Pete 82
semibreve 113
semitones 126
sharps 115, 118, 128
She'll be coming... 108-9
Simon and Garfunkel 60, 70
Simone, Nina 36
slap and tickle 94-5, 96
slide guitar 158-9, 169
Smith, Jimmy 38
staff 112
steel-string (or Western)
    guitar 16-17, 18, 19
straps, guitar 21
Streets of Laredo 78-9
strings 18-19, 22, 30
    bottom and top 30
    cleaning 19
    gauges 18
    restringing 19, 176-7
    winder 176
strumming 12, 44-51
    down stroke 44
    fist and palm strokes 94-5
    regular 48
    smooth 47, 49
    thumb and finger 44-5
    triplets 98-9
    up stroke 45
    sus chords 61, 85, 151
Study No 1 in G 118-19

Study No 1 in Am 120-1
Sweet baby's arms 106-7
Sweet baby James 56
Swing low... 32-3
syncopation 123

tablature (tab) 117, 118-19
Taylor, James 16, 56
tempo 112
theory 126-147
Thompson, Hank 96
'three-chord trick' 131
three-note chords *see* triads
thumb 29, 35, 36, 54
thumb-lead 152-3
'tick-tock' effect 87
time signatures 98, 114, 115
tones 126
Tower of Power 161
Travis, Merle 155
Travis Picking 155
triads 129-30
tuners 21
tuning, of guitar 18, 22-3,177
tunings, alternative 168-9
twelve bar blues 156
    in Am 146-7
    in G 144-5
twelve bar blues in G 144

'up' 30
up stroke 45

Waltzing Matilda 102-3
We shall overcome 46-7
Welch, Gillian 152
Wild Horses 168
Wynette, Tammy 106

Young, Neil 82

CD track listing

To increase the clarity of the 'HOW TO PLAY' tracks on the CD, you can isolate the guitar patterns you will be following by turning off the right channel of your hi-fi or just pan to the left. All other tracks are meant to be heard in stereo.

CD	Track title	Page
1-6	Tuning	22
7	1st chords	31
8-9	Swing Low Sweet Chariot	33
10-11	What Shall We Do with the Drunken Sailor	35
12-13	He's Got the Whole World in his Hands	37
14-15	Down by the Riverside	39
16-17	John Brown's Body	41
18-19	We Shall Overcome	47
20-21	O Sole Mio	49
22-23	Amazing Grace	51
24-25	Oh Susannah	57
26-27	Danny Boy	59
28-29	Scarborough Fair	61
30-31	Cockles and Mussels	63
32-33	All Through the Night	65
34	Alternating bass patterns	66
35-36	Careless Love	69
37-38	Banks of the Ohio	71
39-40	Daisy, Daisy	77
41-42	Streets of Laredo	79
43-44	Home On The Range	83
45-46	Greensleeves	85
47-48	My Grandfather's Clock	87
49-50	Early One Morning	91
51-52	Slapping techniques	94
53-54	Mama Don't Allow	97
55-56	The Irish Washerwoman	99
57-59	Hammer-on, pull-off	100, 101
60-61	Waltzing Matilda	103
62-63	Bass runs in Bluegrass	105
64-65	Rollin' in my Sweet Baby's Arms	107
66-67	She'll Be Coming Round the Mountain	109
68	Study No 1 in G	118
69	Study No 2 in Am	121
70	Gingernut Rag	122
71	The major scale	126
72	Triads in the key of C major	130

CD	Track title	Page
73	The four-note chords for C major	132
74	Sample chord progression	135
75	Minor scales	136
76-78	Other scales	139
79	C pentatonic scale	141
80	Rock and blues 'licks'	142
81	12-bar blues in G	144
82	12-bar blues in Am	146
83	Folk made easy	150
84-85	Country made easy	153,154
86-87	Rock'n'roll made easy	156,157
88	Slide made easy	159
89-90	Funk & reggae made easy	160,161
91	Power chords made easy	164
92-93	Bossa nova made easy	166
94-95	Rumba made easy	167
96-97	Alternative tunings	168,169
98	Danny Boy – Jazz style	173

Acknowledgements

David Harrison and James Harrison would like to thank Penny Woods and Rich Purves at Modern Music, 7/9 High St., Abingdon, OX14 5BB for their friendly help and advice, and for the use of guitars, amps, leads, and other accessories used in this book. A great store - email info@modernmusic.demon.co.uk

Thank you also to the following for their time and effort in modelling and helping the book along: Alison Fields, Leonardo di Lorenzo, David Berger, Billie Suliat Baker, Lenie Mets, Heather McDonough, Dexter Harrison, Rowan Brown, Ben Edwards, Michael Labat, Fiona Nagpal. Apologies to anyone we've left out in error. Patricia Hymans for the index. Duncan Carr for the scans. And a special thank you to Nick Withers for making sound design sense of the music graphics and other horrors hurled at him. Thanks also to Roisin Ni Bhriain at the Irish Traditional Music Archives (www.itma.ie), to Hank's, 24 Denmark Street, London WC2H 8NE (www.wom.co.uk/hanks) and to London Resonator Centre, 44 Duncan Street, London N1 8BW (www.resocentre.com).

Picture credits

All photography by Matthew Ward, except 9 (t), 17 (t) James Harrison; 44-45, 184 David Harrison; 10 (b), 89, 97, 145, 146 151, 152, 155, 157, 158, 159 (tl, tr) 163, 170, 172, Dave Peabody

Music credits

Guitar playing, singing and saxophone on the CD by David Harrison. Recorded by Guy Dagul. Arrangements by Guy Dagul. The study pieces on pages 118,121,122 are © David Harrison.

Publisher's note

⚙ Collins need to know?

Want to know about other popular subjects and activities?
Look out for further titles in Collins' practical and accessible
Need to Know? series.

Digital photography
All the kit, techniques and tips you need to take great photographs

192pp   £8.99
PB   0 00 718031 4

Golf
All the kit, techniques and inspiration to get into the game

192pp   £8.99
PB   0 00 718037 3

Zodiac types
Yourself, your friends and your family revealed

192pp   £7.99
PB   0 00 718038 1

Watercolour
All the kit, techniques and inspiration you need to get into painting

192pp   £8.99
PB   0 00 7189032 2

Card games
All the rules and tips you need to start playing over 60 card games

192pp   £6.99
PB   0 00 719080 8

Yoga
All the tips and techniques to get you healthy in mind and body

192pp   £8.99
PB   0 00 719091 3

Pilates
All the tips and techniques you need to get a flexible body

192pp   £8.99
PB   0 00 719063 8 8

Guitar
All the gear, techniques and tips you need to play the guitar

192pp   £8.99
PB   0 00 719088 3

Forthcoming titles:

Birdwatching
DIY
Drawing & Sketching
Stargazing
Weddings
French
Italian

Spanish
Kama Sutra
Dog Training
Knots & Splices
World Atlas
World Factfile

To order any of these titles,
please telephone **0870 787
1732**. For further information
about all Collins books, visit our
website: **www.collins.co.uk**